JOB INTERVIEW PREPARATION

TECHNIQUES TO OVERCOME ANXIETY, SPEAKING SKILLS, QUESTIONS AND ANSWERS, STEP BY STEP PROCESS

BORIS PARKER

Contents

Introduction

If you're invited for a job interview, then there is a likelihood you possess at least some of the simple skills for the function for which you're to be interviewed. So now what? You have the education, you have the experience, and you have the interview; however, you cannot simply print out your resume and iron your enterprise suit. Even if you are immensely qualified to keep the function for which you are interviewing, preparing to ace that job interview requires that you hone some abilities that are possibly the foundation of your job capabilities set. You may also be asking why job interview coaching is necessary- why can't your resume simply talk for you? As arbitrary and tedious as job interview preparation may feel, you still want to participate. Getting ready for your job interviews gives you the reasons and self-belief to let your proper competencies and work values shine through, and it conveys to your interviewer that you are a serious and competent candidate.

So what does job interview instruction entail? An essential section of job interview coaching is the lookup you can do about your possible employer and the role that you may hopefully be filling.

Internet searches and visits to the library can assist you in determining and understanding the workings, history, and mission of your prospective employer, which in turn may also assist you to focus your experiences (and resume) so that you can design a professional narrative full of applicable points and accomplishments. The research will help you think of significant questions you would possibly have about the employer or position, which you will probably be given a chance to ask at the interview's end.

Interviews are mostly used as a device of evaluation in the hands of the employer. However, candidates also use interviews to examine firms when attempting to decide whether to work for the institution or not. Research on job interviews has confirmed the essence of job interviews in the hiring technique of organizations. By definition, a job interview is a tactical discussion between an applicant and either a representative(s) or an HR professional of the recruiting organization. It is used to evaluate a candidate for a specific job opening inside the organization. Job interviews continue to be one of the most popular tools used in recruitment exercises by organizations.

With the invention of advanced technology and the internet, interviews are no longer confined to face-to-face conversations. They have morphed into more magnificent yet advanced forms. Some of these encompass telephone interviews, online chats, and video calls between employers and manageable employees. Since you're searching for how to ace a job interview, we assume it's only crucial to take a look at all types of interviews you may come upon as a job seeker. Below are the ten types of interviews you could stumble upon as an applicant:

1. Traditional interviews

2. Telephone interviews

3. Lunch interviews

4. Firing squad interviews

5. Skype interviews

6. Puzzle interviews

7. Career honest interviews

8. Case Interviews

9. Apprentice interviews

10. Group interviews

Traditional Interviews

These are face-to-face interviews. You are questions from a representative of the corporation to examine your suitability for the function for which the business enterprise is recruiting.

Telephone Interviews

In telephone interviews, the employer fixes an interview appointment with the applicant over the telephone at a virtually exact time. In most cases, it is commonly a precursor to the regular interview. Provoking the interviewer naturally brings the recruitment exercise to an abrupt end. During phone interviews, strive no longer to be awkward.

Lunch Interviews

There are situations where your possible employer needs to have a direct feel of your personality outside the office.This is a type of interview where you are being asked interviewed and considered for employment because you are expected to represent and embody the organization in an official capacity. Like all interviews, you strive to deliver shrewd answers to questions from the representative of the organization. During lunch interviews, you must be attentive to some things pertaining to your etiquette and mannerisms, which are as follow:

How to order your meal?

Let the interviewer request his/her meal first

Request a meal that will allow you to talk with ease while eating

Be well-mannered when speaking to restaurant staff and waiters

Don't drink or eat too much

Show "Appreciate" after the meal

Avoid crabs, pasta, lobsters, and ingredients with a lot of pepper

Don't order an expensive meal

Avoid alcohol

Maintain an expert aura and tone all through

Firing Squad Interviews

These are interviews where you get interviewed via a group of representatives who would fire questions at you in the way that the name suggests. This type of interviews is often born out of job roles where you would be required to work with a group of individuals who would shape your reporting lines.

In these situations, expectations are high from the employers, but it also helps you because rather than have separate interviews with every unit head, you would have an interview with all of them simultaneously.

Skype Interviews

Skype interviews are starting a natural form of an interview for firms that choose to take full benefit of technological offerings. You should, however, have it in mind that while a Skype interview would possibly save you the stress of going to the physical workplace of the recruiting company, it is one that needs to be navigated with caution. For instance, to have a profitable Skype Interview, you ought to make certain that your laptop, smartphone or any gadget you intend to use has enough battery power to last the duration of the interview.

You wouldn't be considered as professional and ready to work if your laptop shut down in the middle of an interview. Also, you should ensure your internet connection is strong enough to warranty an internet connection for the period of the interview. You must also be excellently dressed and hold your mannerisms professional all through the period of the interview.

Puzzle Interviews

Puzzle interviews without difficulty stand out as one of the most dreaded types of interviews for candidates, and the cause is simple; the nature of questions you are asked at puzzle interviews can throw a spanner into all the work you have put into the preparation. An instance is getting to the venue of an interview, and upon sitting in the front of your interviewer, you are asked this question:

"You're standing opposite two doors. One of the doorways leads to Heaven, while the second, leads to Hell. In front of every door stand two angels. One of the angels always speaks the fact while the other usually lies, but you have no idea of which of them is the liar and which is the trustworthy messenger. To get to Paradise, you are only permitted to ask one of the angels a question.

What question would you ask?" How would you reply to this? The solution is now not an exact answer. Rather, the interviewer is really interested in your reasoning potential and your strategy for finding solutions to challenges and situations.

The top-secret of succeeding at this type of interview is to be calm, identify what the problem is, and then channel your effort into breaking down the question/puzzle to bits and pieces. There are two matters you should keep away from all through puzzle interviews – First, you must face up to the temptation of panicking. Secondly, do now not fall into the error of throwing a collection of questions at the interviewer. Ask reasonable yet restrained questions by showing your prospective organization how your thought pattern works when faced with different situations and challenges.

Career Fair Interviews

Career fairs are high opportunities to galvanize your possible employer. Interviews held at career gala's offer you at most, 10-15 minutes to promote yourself and make your interviewer see your potentials. As you would possibly have guessed, this virtual capability you have to put your satisfactory foot ahead to get invited to a more problematic interview.

Below is a listing of pointers to help you excel at a career fair interview:

i.   Keep your dressing smart and formal

ii. Go alongside with a hard and smooth copy of your CV and other credentials.

iii. Take advantage of the chance to network.

iv. Maintain a strong and confident body language.

v.   Keep your breath fresh.

vi. Prepare a verbal commercial enterprise card (about 45 seconds long).

Case Interviews

In 'case interviews,' possible personnel are given a real-life case study to work on.

As an example, a recruiting corporation ought to be hiring for the position of a content material marketer and present a case study, which indicates that the advertising group sends out one email publication on a weekly basis to its subscribers database but isn't accumulating adequate leads for the Sales Departments, and you're asked to offer suggestion. You are then anticipated to endorse techniques that may want to help yield extra leads as a solution.

As feedback, you ought to propose that the employer looks in the path of paid Ads with a well-cantered target audience and budget. You could also propose that the organization amplify the quantity of email e-newsletter depending on the wide variety of products and offerings in focus.

Apprentice Interviews

For apprentice interviews, your prospective employer is not the type that can be impressed with listening to what someone can do or your past accomplishments. Rather, your interviewer, in this case, desires to see what you can do. For instance, if the position is for a Recruitment Consultant, your interviewee could sit down with you in a real-life interview with graduate intern to see how desirable you are at examining candidates. Apprentice interviews allow you to shine. So, make fantastic use of the opportunity.

Group Interviews

These are interviews where the hiring corporation interviews candidates in groups. In this kind of interview, a candidate would locate himself/herself being interviewed along with five other applicants or more depending on the preference of the company. This type of interview is extra commonplace for roles round income jobs and internships. It ought to prove a bit complex for candidates who are on the shy side; however, with a bit preparation, you can ace it.

One odd trait of group interviews is that it comes as a surprise to candidates, especially those who are not prepared for it. In some team interviews, you will be interviewed inside as a group or as a crew and would possibly even be interviewed by a team of interviewers.

The trick is to continue to be assured and answer the questions as they are thrown at you. Group interviews are also recognized to existing you with case studies the place your interviewer(s) will examine you on how you interact with others, your degree of inclination in the direction of problem-solving reasoning, self-belief and how you react to conditions that name for the utility of your skill-set and experience.

To shine in a crew interview, you must attempt now not to show up, amazed when you stroll into the interview and discover that you do not have a one-on-one interview. Regardless of how amazed you might be, do now not let this reaction locate its way to your face. Maintain self-confidently. At group interviews, it's crucial to make friends. If you arrive for the interview at the right time, possibilities are that the chance to have interaction with other candidates before the interview will present itself. When it does, sink your enamel into it; ask for their names, begin conversations with them. Some interviewers note this, and it is bound to leave a good impression.

At group interviews, the truth that you already had a dialogue with other candidates will push your self-assurance and familiarity with their names a couple of notches higher. Finally, throughout group interviews, you desire to continue to be yourself, pay attention to what others have to say, and get all individuals involved. Remember not to come throughout as too overbearing in your attempt to lead the conversations. This has strong tendencies to backfire.

CHAPTER ONE

How to Find the Right Job

Building a career is a real hassle these days, and the success of our endeavors has been intently related to our capacity to locate the fabulous sphere of pastime and action. Therefore, we can say that growing a profession depends very much on the job we operate genuinely. That is because searching for a job is an exercise that can outline our abilities. Imagine the gap between the description of the to-do list of a physician and the actual skills of a lawyer. Similarly, any person who chooses a particular type of job, however, must have the skills to function well in that field. If he doesn't he is likely to fail because he can't put into practice his skills and what he outlined in his resumes, predominant assets and the fellow will be spending his energy inefficiently on tasks that are not rewarding to him or the company in any way.

Thus, it is essentially important to find a job that fits your interests and performance. There is a vast array of picks that we can take so that we will set the foundation for our future career effectively. We can identify such opportunities even in high-school when we begin concentrating on a unique sphere of activity. Furthermore, we can have a look at the analogies between our innate abilities and viable careers in nowadays labor market. Career counseling is the 2nd choice, and, in general, this professional help would possibly be explored in the university and after graduation. Continuing schooling is the 1/3 practicable alternative and helps you enhance understanding through particular trainings.

Do you ever query whether or not you're on the right profession path? I went through a radical career shift in my early 20s when I went from counterterrorism specialist to career coach! It was hard realizing that the career I had spent so long building wasn't really right for me, but sincerely finding my proper route was once so profoundly satisfying. And I'm no longer by myself in making that change. In the US, about 33% are currently thinking about a career change, while about 75% have changed careers at least once. Finding your desired profession won't happen overnight, and it might also take time to discover the right trajectory for you. You would possibly even be thinking,

"How do I even know what the proper profession is?"

Luckily, I've been there, and I'm right here to assist!

If you're unsure, feeling stuck, or confused, worry less. Here are steps you can take to discover the career that will justly fulfill you.

Take career assessments.

Do you remember, in school, being given career persona checks that would inform you what you be when you develop up? They may additionally have appeared silly; however, the proper career assessment can virtually be a particularly useful device in discovering your path, mainly if you aren't sure where to start. There are two factors to a professional assessment.

- It should be valid and reliable. The check must genuinely measure what it claims to measure, and you need to get constant outcomes over more than one tries.

- You should know how to use the effects to your advantage. It's one factor to have a list of plausible careers. It's some other to use a career evaluation as a beginning point for perception and self-reflection. Remember, a professional evaluation isn't a shortcut; it's a tool. It's up to you to use it.

Make a list of your options.

Have you overwhelmed via the need to make a decision? Whether you understand what you want to do or not, understanding how to get there is tricky. To locate your dream career, you need to carefully search and research your options to find a great direction you can take.

Make a list of all your choices, whether those are palpable job openings, career paths, or education. When you have the whole lot written down, you can analyze what isn't precisely right, and trim down your options to match your goals. Try to create as many alternatives for yourself, so you have plenty to pick from. You can additionally rank your choices from pleasant to worst, and even mix some that might also be similar.

Look for overlap.

What you're properly good at, what companies need, and what you like to do might all be different; however, it's vital to try to locate the overlap between the three. That's how you discover your most reliable career path. Rather than looking at job titles, reflect on consideration of your interests, hobbies, and skills, and then make your choice. While you're at it, look again at your previous experiences to inform your future. What did you experience doing in previous jobs? What did you dislike? Knowing your values, passions, and abilities will help you recognize what sort of career you would trail. And being watchful of these features means you can be looking for careers that require your unique talents.

Network.

Whether you're actively looking out for a new career, or just attempting to get a feel of what route you be on, networking is an excellent way to dip your fit in the waters. The more human beings you meet, the greater the insight you can get into what the work environment is like, what the people are like, and how they experience the work. And if you are looking for that subsequent job, networking is crucial. Surveys exhibit about 85% of jobs are got through networking!

Ask a mentor.

Never underestimate the cost and strength of a correct tutor! When I completed my career change, I knew I couldn't do it unaccompanied. I determined I wanted to learn from the fine — so I started working with mentors. There are many different sorts of mentors, from the form you pay to those that have been there, done that, to the type that can guide you at work: the right mentor, no count number what type, will supply you practice and assist your career. And the research backs it up — about 80% of CEOs attribute their success to having labored with mentors.

Trust me — I comprehend discovering your dream profession isn't easy, and the course can be scary. But only because it's difficult doesn't imply it's not worth it! Think about how a lot of time you'll spend at work in your lifetime — 90,000 hours for the average person. You want to make certain you're using your time to your advantage by using trailing a career that pleases you, utilizes your talents, aligns with your standards, and more. You have the control to attain it, and now you have the gears to get started. Are you set?

CHAPTER TWO

The Speaking Skills that Make You the Right Person for the Job

Discussing your strengths and shortcomings can be one of the most challenging components of the job interview. Avoid interview paralysis with my advice. If you were ever asked the query "What are your strengths and faintness?" in a job interview, you in all likelihood right away noticed your heart racing. How do I say what I'm now not precise at barring searching horrible and say what I am suitable at bragging? Yep, this is a toughie. But there may be a secret formula that can help you succeed: Emphasize an excellent exceptional or talent; this is wished for the job, and minimize—but be truthful about—the negatives.

Let's say, two candidates—we'll call them Sarah and Norman—have job interviews for a customer carrier manager position. As always, one of the interview questions they will be requested is about their strengths and weaknesses.

First up is Sarah. When she's asked, "What are your biggest strengths and weaknesses?" Sarah responds, "My energy is that I'm a difficult worker. My weakness is that I get confused when I pass over a cut-off date because someone else dropped the ball."

This reply is unimaginative, a no-brainer. Most human beings assume of themselves as difficult workers—who would genuinely admit to no longer being a difficult worker? Also, Sarah's weakness is technically not a weakness, plus she passes the buck: Someone—not he—drops the ball, which causes her to get stressed.

Now it is Norman's turn. He also has a challenge with the question. "I honestly cannot think of a weakness," he begins. "Maybe I could be more focused. My strength is possibly my capacity to deal with people. I am extraordinarily easy-going. I generally do not get upset easily."

This reply leads with a negative and then strikes to vague words: maybe, probably, relatively and usually. Norman isn't always doing himself any favors.

So what is the best way to reply to this common interview question?

Evaluating your Weaknesses

How about we get the intense eliminate of the way first—your shortcomings. This is likely the most feared area of the inquiry. Everybody has flaws, however, who wants to admit to them, particularly in a meeting?

A few instances of shortcomings you may reference include:

i.   Attempting to satisfy everybody

ii. Being new to the ultra-present-day programming

iii. Being excessively crucial of yourself

An ideal approach to adapt to this inquiry is to diminish the quality and underline the positive. Select a characteristic and think of a response to defeat your shortcomings. Avoid individual characteristics and listen more to expert attributes.

Evaluating your Strengths

When it comes to time to evaluate yourself, you should be explicit. Survey your abilities to find your qualities. This practice is worth doing before any meeting. Make a rundown of your aptitudes, isolating them into three classes:

Information based aptitudes: Acquired from training and adventure (e.g., PC canny, dialects, degrees, instruction, and specialized capacity).

Transferable aptitudes: Your transportable capabilities that you take from employment to work (e.g., discussion abilities, expository issue fixing and arranging skills)

Individual characteristics: Your unique qualities (e.g., being reliable, adaptable, amicable, persevering, expressive, formal, timely, and a team player).

A few instances of strengths you may specify include:

1. Creativity

2. Enthusiasm

3. Trustworthiness

4. Respectfulness

5. Discipline

6. Willpower

7. Patience

8. Honesty

9. Versatility

10. Dedication

Choose three to five of these qualities that match the business activity you are venturing into. You must be able to give reasons you included those skills you included in your resume and defend them when the time is right. .

Scripting your answers

When you're mentioned to show your qualities, be mindful about establishing the correct pace. A few questioners may likewise request that you "gloat a little about yourself." In responses, you'll like to show a thoughtful fearlessness – not one or the other "concealing your light underneath a bushel" nor putting on a show of being excessively egotistic.

The incredible system is to practice arrangements about your qualities before the meeting, setting aside this effort to map out how you can "sell" these strengths will help businesses' needs in an exceptional case. This gives you an insight into the business, showing how you would be a team player.

Compose an incredible proclamation you can say with certainty:

"My strength is my capability to deal with change. As a customer transporter director at my last occupation, I had the option to turn around a poor workplace and build up a powerful group. For my shortcomings, I realize that my abilities ought to be more grounded, and I am constantly attempting to improve them."

At the moment when gone up against with this inquiry question, remember the questioner is searching for a fit. She is framing an image of your dependents on your answers. A single answer will likely never again save you from landing the position, except if it is something outright. Put your capacity into your quality's articulation— what you bring to the table. At that point, let the interviewers know that you can be perfect, let them know you are dealing with any weaknesses you have.

1

Try not to be hesitant to act naturally. Demonstrating a portion of your character can be a good thought during the interview. It will assist the interviewer with learning increasingly about you as an individual and will enable you to talk eagerly about your expert advantages and aptitudes.

- • Maintain proficient discourse at whatever point you are looking at anything individual.

- • Don't broadly expound if discussing yourself, going through just around one moment doing as such.

2

Attempt to relate individual subtleties to the necessities of the job. At the point when you talk about any close to home subjects, you can relate them to aptitudes that are applicable to the position you are being interviewed for. This will enable you to express both your character and show your aptitudes and experience.

- You could discuss how you showed yourself a language or instrument to delineate that you can adapt to new abilities and procedures.

- Discussing how you sorted out a network occasion can embody your authority aptitudes

3

Act, talk, and dress professionally. During the interview it will be essential that you demonstrate, talk and dress moderately. By introducing yourself as a skilled and genuine candidate you will be bound to establish a decent first connection. Wearing clothes fitting to the position that you are interviewing for is compulsory for an effective interview.

- Make sure you are dressed suitably for your interview. Ask your contact at the organization what the dress code resembles where you are interviewing.

- Men should wear a shirt and slacks. Ladies can wear a dress shirt or pullover with a skirt at any knee-length.

- Don't use any slang or expressions. Talking like you would with companions or family is unreasonably easygoing for a job interview.

- Avoid utilizing any filler words like "um" or "uh." It's necessary to make your discourse open-ended.

4

Express abilities that employers are searching for. During the interview, you will need to show that you have the right stuff and abilities that your employer is searching for. Numerous potential employers search for comparative skills during the interview. Audit the accompanying rundown of aptitudes that you can examine during the interview:

- Possession of relational abilities. This can be exhibited throughout the interview.

- Be knowledgable about the organization. Research the organization and think about some ideas or questions you can raise.

- Be skilled and innovative. Try not to be hesitant to talk about your capacities with standard innovation aptitudes, for example, word processors or any specific projects.

- You must be able to oversee assets. Discover a period in your vocation that will outline your capacity to work with a spending limit.

- Be adaptable to new circumstances. Talk about a period in your expert life when you had the option to discover achievement in any event, during a period of progress.

- Be authoritative. Delineate a period in your last position when you were a pioneer, concentrating on what you gained from it.

5

Know about your non-verbal communication. A greater part of the interview will be verbal. Be that as it may, there will likewise be information passed on using non-verbal communication. Give careful consideration to your non-verbal communications to establish an extraordinary connection during your interview.

- Appear confident and quiet.

- Avoid yawning or seeming occupied.

- Make eye to eye connection and smile once in a while to show a positive mindset.

- Don't neglect to relax. Holding your breath or breathing an excess of air can be interpreted as an absence of certainty.

6

Remain positive. At the point when you are examining any theme or responding to an inquiry during the interview, you ought to consistently concentrate your reaction on positive perspectives. Keeping the interview on the best parts of yourself and your circumstance can expand your odds of getting the job.

- If a negative address or detail comes up, talk about its positive parts.

- Framing a disappointment as a learning experience can be a decent method to remain positive.

- Instead of whining about a troublesome time, portray how it made you an increasingly proficient individual.

- Even if a unique objective didn't work out, you can outline your flexibility and how you had the option to function with change.

7

Listen cautiously. You will need to deliberately tune in to anything your interviewer says during the interview. Giving careful consideration will assist you in responding to questions. Taking in subtleties of the discussion can likewise help you with thinking about any inquiries you may have for the interviewer.

- Avoid reacting to issue while the interviewer is talking. Hold on until they are finished talking before you react to them.

- Listening attentively will give you a chance to hear subtleties that may have been missed generally.

Fantastic relational abilities are basic for the working environment. After you've been interviewed, try to ask interviewers about how you comport, convey yourself, and to have your capacity to impart in the working environment tried and assessed. Despite the job, employers look for employees who can coexist with others and who can impart well both verbally and non-verbally.

At the point when you interview for a job, the contracting chief will get some information about relational abilities, including how you address issues, how you handle testing circumstances, what you expect similar to correspondence from the executives, and different inquiries identified with your capacity to convey.

Peruse underneath for proposals on the best way to react to interview inquiries concerning interchanges, just as test answers to basic inquiries.

What the Interviewer Will search For

Notwithstanding the reactions you give, your capacity to convey will be assessed. What are your verbal and nonverbal relational abilities? How well do you clarify your answers? How expressive would you say you are? Do you listen cautiously to what the interviewers are stating, or do you hinder and attempt to rule the discussion? Do you look at your interviewers without flinching when you address them? What does your non-verbal communication state about you?

When interviewers pose their questions, they do so not only to pick up information from you but to also know how you convey your thoughts through verbal tone and nonverbal gesticulations and paralinguistic cues.

Here are some abilities the hiring manager will assess:

1. Listening

2. Confidence

3. Empathy

4. Friendliness (would you say you are anything but difficult to converse with?)

5. Nonverbal cues(do you give off an impression of being pushed or awkward?)

6. Respect

7. How clear and compact your reactions are

STEP BY STEP GUIDE ON HOW TO ANSWER QUESTIONS ABOUT COMMUNICATIONS

Interviewing can come in any form for the best communicator. Reacting formally and clearly to questions implies accomplishing a harmony between tuning in to what the interviewer is asking, and giving a well-considered reaction to questions.

If you have to catch up on your interviewing abilities, ensure you rehearse before a mirror or friends. As I said earlier, hone your interviewing skills by using a partner, spouse, sibling, companion or friend, or anybody that you are comfortable when you are around them. You can even do it independently away from the eye of anyone else – you can do that before a mirror. Despite the fact that it is anything but a "genuine" interview, you'll have the option to consider, ahead of time, how you will react and how you will sync with your interviewers.

Correspondence Interview Questions

Plan ahead of time by inspecting these interview questions and instances of the best answers about correspondence will help you in detailing your one of a kind reactions.

- Do you function admirably with other individuals?

- Tell me about yourself.

- How would you describe yourself?

- What significant difficulties, challenges and issues have you ever faced and successfully aced? How did you handle them?

- Describe a challenging work circumstance/venture and how you overcame it.

- What have you gained from your experience?

- What would it say it looked like working for your former manager?

- What do you expect from an administrator?

- How would you handle pressure?

- What has been the biggest dissatisfaction in your life?

- What would you say you are good at?

- What are your turn-offs?

- What do people regularly reprimand about you?

- When last were you angry? What caused it?

- Will you like to work independently or in a group?

- Give a few instances of your collaboration in finishing a basic undertaking.

- Why would you say you are the most ideally equipped individual for the job?

- Why would you like to work here?

- What would you add to this organization?

Instances of the Best Answers

Here are a couple of test answers to different interview inquiries concerning your relational abilities. As you rehearse and practice your very own responses to these inquiries, recollect that your appearance, eye to eye connection, and manner of communicating are as significant as the appropriate responses themselves.

CHAPTER THREE

Recruitment Agencies

You would possibly have a kick-ass CV and attractive cover letter, however looking for those roles and bagging an interview is a serious task. Recruitment agencies would possibly sound esoteric and scary, but they can critically accelerate the procedure! Most people assume that recruitment agencies are meant for those in senior positions; however, recruiters can surely assist you to discover full-time, part-time, or temping opportunities, no matter what stage of your profession you are.

But at some stages in your career, having the proper humans guiding you via your job search can make all the distinction when it comes to finding the appropriate role. And one of the excellent sources you can take gain of is recruitment agencies.

Not sure how they really work? Here's a piece of information about the recruitment agencies, and a few recommendations to get you started:

How do recruitment agencies work?

Recruitment businesses genuinely exist to assist agencies in filling for vacancies in order to aid you in finding employment. Huge organizations, in particular, don't have time to look through thousands of CVs and pick the best candidates for interviews, especially, when they are hiring for plenty of positions.

This is where the recruitment agencies come in – when a corporation gets in contact with them about a new job role, they shall pick out the exceptional candidates on their books to put forward for the interview — recruiters save corporation's lots of time and effort by only putting forward top quality, appropriate applicants. More so, recruiters assist candidates in getting these interviews with the aid of optimizing their CVs or teaching them for interviews. In a nutshell, recruitment corporations are the middle man between the candidates and companies.

Do recruitment agencies take a fee from your salary?

So you would possibly be thinking about how recruitment organizations really make any money out of this – what's in it for them?

First of all, you don't have to pay to use a recruitment company – they're completely free for job seekers. It's the employers who pay the recruitment business enterprise to find the required staff. And how exactly they get paid varies based on the type of position.

Provisional roles – If the event you contact a recruitment agency to find is successful, it's in all likelihood your income will come directly from the recruitment agency itself, rather than from your employer. The recruiters get this money from the employer (their charge for filling the roles), and then they throw it on to you as pay – but of course, they'll keep a cut for themselves. This would not necessarily imply you may get paid less, and it is just that the amount they get paid from the organization is sufficient to cover the whole workers' salary and their charges.

Lasting roles – For most permanent roles, the recruitment organization will be paid when a candidate is hired. They'll usually get paid 15–20% of your starting salary. Importantly though, this cash does not come out of your salary, it's more cash that your company pays to the recruitment employer on top of your wage.

The benefits and negative aspects of recruitment agencies

What's so gorgeous about recruitment agencies? Why should you think of contacting them, instead of simply searching for yourself?

Advantages

Agencies have jobs you may not locate elsewhere

Many agencies pick out recruitment companies as their sole technique of finding new workers. This is because they prefer paying recruitment businesses to do the tough phase of sifting through lots of CVs to put collectively a shortlist of candidates for them, as averse to doing it themselves. Therefore, you are in all likelihood to hear about vacancies from recruiters that you have not seen marketed someplace else – despite observing each job site like a hawk!

You'll get professional instruction from a professional

When contacting an agency, you'll be allotted a recruiter who needs to understand the entirety there is to understand about the job market you are interested in (try testing them if you favor being sure!). They'll be able to give hundreds of information, consisting of where the exceptional jobs are that match your resume, profile, skills. The information will be all about the unique attributes and skills employers are searching for, and even whether or not your skills and qualifications are up to the basics of what they are looking for. If not, start working on restructuring your resume!

Most agencies only get paid when you get the job.

This capacity that you can rest assured that they may do their best to make positive that you at least get an interview because that's the only way they may be eventually get paid! To extend your possibilities of success, they shall regularly provide to improve your CV and educate you for interviews. They simply want you to get the job as you also hope you could, so having that extra support is a fantastic bonus in a competitive job market.

Potential for More Options

Staffing companies represent a couple of agencies so most are amalgamation of many companies. This potential that with one utility you have to get entry to a wider range and quantity of positions that you ought to potentially be a match for. It's frequent for staffing agencies to send candidates for multiple interviews. The more interviews you have, the better your chances of getting your next job. Even if they don't have the right role for you at the time, their stock of jobs is constantly changing. The role you are searching for might also come handy day after today, and you will be the first to be considered for it.

Only Apply for Serious Companies Looking to Hire

Recruiters at staffing companies have their fingers on the pulse of the job market all the time. They are aware of who is hiring and what the positions maintain in phrases of future growth. The professional organizations will only work with those groups that they know to be suitable employers as well. Just as they have checked their candidates, they have additionally vetted their consumer businesses. You can have peace of thinking to understand that you have anyone advocating for you and on your side.

Representatives Are Motivated to Get You Placed

It is the recruiter's job to vicinity candidates and fills open positions. Because they work for each of the candidates and the businesses, they are fantastically inspired to meet the wishes of both. Their purpose is to make the proper placement the first time for their consumers (or at least it has to be). They will work to put you in front of the quality organizations that fit your job search goals.

Disadvantages

Don't get us wrong, businesses additionally have their downsides – and over the years the enterprise has gotten a bit of a horrific rep. You must be taking benefit of what groups offer; however, we would not propose relying on them as your only structure of job search. Here's why.

Recruitment companies don't cover every job and industry.

Some corporations decide not to use recruiting companies – if you've been doing a lot of jobs looking yourself, you may be used to seeing the 'no vacancies please' message at the end of job postings. If you are working with an organization that only has a few openings at a time or specializes in an industry that is no longer your chosen field, you may additionally restriction your options. You will do yourself good by positively portraying the company you work with. That symbolizes the form of employers and industries you are interested in and that they work with a giant quantity of groups, so you have more plausible options.

This is because some corporations choose to do their stuff and don't prefer to pay organizations for work. They're pleased to do themselves. It's proper that some additionally see recruiters as solely being in it for themselves, and as a result, do not believe their judgment when it comes to discovering them the right candidate for the job. So, if you are the use of companies as your only job source, you may want to be lacking out on a job that would be best for you.

Agents have a lot of pinnacle intelligence on their books.

Now job market is more aggressive than ever, so it's truthful to say that you may be up against candidates with some great skills and experience. Some organizations may put an extra cost on higher-level candidates. If you're now not one, you ought to be pushed to the back burner. Make a positive contribution that the company you apply to will have no choice but to create a position for you. You must also see opportunities in every situation, in the fields you are certified and ensure that you showcase your best so you are considered for employment in the future.

This does not imply you won't be successful; it is simply about skills that you need to spread your wings a little bit and seem into all available selections. If you are feeling much less confident, why not spend a bit of time gaining new and needed experience to improve your prospects?

They might not always be straightforward.

So, we're not saying that recruiters lie well, we are, kind of. This is ,though, no skill the case for every recruitment agency, but it is worth being conscious that some will bend the truth a little to gain your interest in a role (as this makes them look like they're doing a proper job).

For example, an agency may draw you in by using mentioning a high revenue for a unique position, solely to inform you after you've got been provided with the job that the earnings are a good deal lower due to your "lack of ideas a graduate." They do this in the optimism that, as you've now come this far, you will receive the lower salary offer anyway which is for sure quite demanding.

Most agencies only get paid when you get the job

Now you may be questioning – didn't you just say this was an advantage? You're correct on that one; however, it is really due to the fact this point is both right and terrible for job hunters. The fact that the agency only gets paid when they vicinity you in an employer can additionally have its drawbacks. It can suggest they center of attention too an awful lot on making that 'sale' – they see you like a product that they're trying to sell to companies. Some may try and throw you into any job possible except taking the time to know if you're the right fit. Be cautious of this!

How to Find a Good Recruitment Agency?

The excessive streets are chock full of agencies, and as with any aggressive environment, some organizations are higher than others. It's undoubtedly really worth contacting all of the primary businesses to get the ball rolling, then to choose the ones most suitable to you, ask the following essential questions:

How do their approaches work?

At the very least, you have to count on a casual smartphone interview or a chat with your recruiter – if now not a face-to-face assembly to talk about your capabilities and goals. If all you get is a suspiciously conventional electronic mail (aka auto-reply), there may be a danger they will just shove your CV onto a pile and never get to be aware of you. These types of companies see candidates as numbers as an alternative than real talent and don't seem to be worth your time.

Do they know about your industry?

Some companies specialize in positive areas, while others would possibly cover a bit of everything. For example, one organization might be the high-quality shout if you're looking for a job in the advertising and marketing industry, while another would possibly be true for assisting you in supplying brief admin work. Your satisfactory wager is to do a little bit of research earlier than identifying who to reach out to. If you prefer to work in a niche role, make positive your recruiter understands that area. If they don't, they will have a tough time matching you to work that you are fascinated in.

Are they open to students and graduates?

There are some groups out there who cater entirely for college students and graduates, while others are open to them; however, they do not entirely cater to the youth. However, some recruiters may not take on college students or graduates at all, so take a look at the specifics earlier than getting in touch with them!

What if I see a function marketed by way of a recruitment agency?

Recruitment corporations advertise many of their vacancies online. Anyone is capable of applying for these positions, though it doesn't necessarily suggest you'll be signing up to the organization as a result. And, even though the roles they promote will be working for different companies, many of them won't nation the company name until you reach the interview stage.

How awful does the usage of a recruitment organization cost?

You must by no means be charged to use a recruitment agency. Consultants are paid by way of of the employers and acquire their rate based totally on whether you've efficiently begun in a role. There should be no payment without delay from the person.

What next once I secure a job?

The moment you got the job, the role of your organization doesn't end there. They'll handle all of the bureaucracy and different formalities and liaise with your new business enterprise to make sure the whole thing is in order for your first day and beyond. They can even negotiate your income for you and make positive you get the best package out there.

Essentially, it's in their interest to ensure they find a position that's proper for you – and make it as convenient as viable for you to apply, and get started. Job seeking can be a lonely process, but it will become such an awful lot much less so when you're with a recruitment agency.

While there are some downsides to the use of a staffing agency, they can all be averted with aid of making sure you choose the right one to represent you. Do your research, ask around, and make sure you are choosing the corporation with the best popularity and the most jobs. Working with a staffing enterprise to find your next profession will solely help you make wider your options. Employers are the usage of staffing groups, and you be too.

Develop the pinnacle interview manners from HR

If you are seeking job interview success tips, you will gain from the data contained within this career guide. A job interview is a meeting between an attainable worker and a sure enterprise that approves the men and women involved to examine facts on one another. Your purpose as a professional is to display the strengths that you have that will make contributions to the enterprise that you are in search of employment from in an advantageous manner. You will characterize the written records that you have placed on your resume. You will supply your resume which will highlight your personality and character. Here, you will be furnished with the pinnacle five suggestions to ensure that you are successful in the job interview that you have been invited to take attend.

CHAPTER FOUR

12 Tips to Hone Your Job Interview Etiquette

1. Greet your interviewers as Ms or Mr

Most people prefer you to call them by their first name. When was the remaining time any person urged you to call them by their last name?

So, what's the big deal? Well, it's not an exhibit stopper, and there is a minimal hazard you may offend any individual if you do call them by using their first name; however, when you name any person by their last name, you are showing them respect. In essence, you are saying to them, and I appreciate you, and you are important.

Do you like to be respected and to feel important?

Again, it's a little thing, however in a world the place there is too little respect going around, it will make you distinct from competing candidates for this equal role.

Super Tips: Throughout your interview, hiring managers will be attempting to assess how seamlessly you can work with others as a team or manage other people in your team. It's true, employers want self-starters and leaders, but every now and then they certainly want you to be an appropriate soldier and do your job.

2. Ensure your mobile device is off...not on silence mode or vibration

The last thing you need is a distraction at some stage in one of the most necessary meetings of your life. People can nonetheless hear your mobile ring on vibration. You can simply leave your cell phone in the car.

At this moment, your interview is your topmost priority. This should be a life-changing moment for you and your family. BTW--How did we live on all these years besides mobile phones?

3. Look humans in the eye and smile

Body language is an extraordinarily necessary detail of suited job interview etiquette. Communication specialists inform us that 80% of our communication with others is non-verbal. One of the quality approaches to connect with humans and build faith is to look them in the eye. Eye contact is also important for a team interview.

Throughout my government recruiting career, I've once in a while had candidates arrive at a business enterprise wondering why they would be having a one-on-one interview setting, solely to be accompanied into a meeting room with 3 to 4 hiring authorities asking them questions one by one. Most people, when they're below pressure, do not smile, and appear nervous and missing in confidence. It's tremendous how something as simple as a smile can task self-assurance and leadership...even if you're a nervous wreck. Have you ever heard anyone say, I did not have faith that guy? He did not seem to maintain eye contact?! This is very important as it makes the other person sees you as truthful and real.

True Confession: One of my flaws is I tend to have a serious resting face. The reason I'm aware of this is that over the years I've had co-workers, colleagues and friends ask me on several occasions if everything is alright or if I'm upset about something. I use to get aggravated when humans asked me this because most of the time I'm in a proper mood; but, knowing how others interpret my body language offers me the opportunity to overcompensate for this persona quirk whenever I meet new people, supply a speech, or take part in an important meeting.

4. Firm handshake

This is some other non-verbal way to connect with people. It seems ludicrous to be judged negatively via a limp handshake; however, human beings mostly do it. More so, be cautious with this advice. If you're man, don't offer a firm handshake when shaking arms with a woman.There is this man at my church who practically breaks my hand each time we shake hands.I genuinely strive to avoid "The Bone Crusher" on Sunday. He's a wonderful guy, but sheesh, take it easy!

5. Let the company take the lead all through your interview

Sometimes when your interviewer is a soft-spoken or laid back type of person, you may additionally experience the urge to preserve things moving. So, you start taking lower back some manipulate and the next factor you know, you're rambling.

Resist this. Let the corporation run the show.

If there are durations of decorum, just sit there silently. If you've made adequate preparation for the interview, calm, you have nothing to fear about. One of the most frequent interviewing mistakes is speaking too much. It's handy to ramble and over-explain things if your interview is a character of few words, and there are periods of silence. Resist this and truly let them set the tempo of the interview.

6. Don't step on the final three phrases of a persons' conversation

I've noticed a disturbing trend these days.

When I'm speaking with someone, regularly instances they will step on the final 2-3 phrases of my sentence and discuss over me except extending to me the courtesy of ending my sentence.

Has this ever happen to you?

Reporters and TV discuss show hosts do it all the time. It is especially frequent among Type A personalities.

Allow the interviewer to finish making their point, pause for 1-2 seconds; then, add to the conversation or respond to their query.

Check out my job interview readiness quiz. It exposes your shortcomings about the interview manner and reveals how fine to answer.

7. Sit up straight and lean slightly forward

In my function as an executive recruiter, I cannot tell you the variety of instances hiring managers have rejected precise candidates because they had been too laid lower back in their interview literally. This is mainly true for candidates over 50 years old.

Disgracefully, older job seekers are frequently prejudged as lacking in force and ambition; however, youthful job seekers want to also be on protecting in opposition to being too casual or relaxed.

Sitting up straight and leaning slightly ahead sends the accompanying non-verbal sign: I'm listening eagerly. I'm keen on what you need to state. I have a great deal of vitality, and I'm all set to work.

It's challenging to accept as true with that in a few seconds you can make this kind of impression, but it is true. So, pass this slice of interview etiquette at your peril.

8. Take notes during your interview

Bring a professional binder along with you so you can jot down a few notes at some stage in the interview. This passes on a true enthusiasm for what your interviewers need to state and gives you an opportunity to jot down a question to ask lat the right time.

When I say an expert searching binder, I'm no longer speaking about a low-priced three-ring binder like you carried around to the 8th grade. Invest in a leather-based binder that looks, first class. Additionally, don't utilize an iPad or electronic tablet to take notes.

The different excellent issue about having a professional binder on your lap is you can use it as a cheat sheet only if you are nervous. Before your interview, you have to have a few key phrases written down to assist you if you get stuck and you're shortlisted of fabulous questions to ask them. Lastly, you can make available your expert references and copies of your resume in case they ask you for them. If a hiring supervisor asks you for your professional references during your interview, that is a positive signal.

9. Pursue the job even if your performance in the interview is going poorly

You might be enduring a lousy interview journey thinking to yourself, this is the final place I'd ever attend for interview if I ever get out of here. The best recommendation I can supply you is being professional and end what you started out to the exceptional of your capability. Nobody has a weapon to your head to take this job. You're in the driver's seat due to the fact you can continually withdraw from the system or turn down an offer. Here are two situations where job seekers made the deadly mistake of prejudging things too early and lived to regret it. As a universal rule, wait until you have all the information before making your remaining judgment about an individual or a company.

Pearl of Wisdom: You never be aware of who you are going to meet or how a complete stranger would possibly positively affect your career downstream. Leave people with a favorable impact on you. It could pay dividends in the future.

10. Your interview is no longer over until you drive down the road.

 In a few cases, I've recognized hiring managers to look at candidates from their office window as they leave the building and get into their car. People can do some notably ignoble things like spitting, lighting fixtures up a cigarette, arranging themselves, yapping on their cell phone for 20 minutes while leaning on their car, chowing down on a sandwich in their car, and different matters you would no longer believe.

So, continue to be in expert mode till your tail lights are out of sight. Also, you can also be discovered on getting to your interview.

Life Story: One time, a candidate parked his automobile and took a walk from the parking to where the interview was to take place. The building used to be very modern-day and had mirrored glass. You could without difficulty see out of the office.

As the candidate approached the entrance, he shortly darted over in the front of one of the mirrored windows adjoining to the door to do a closing minute check of his look and pull a few hairs out of place.

So he proceeded to spit in his hand, rub them together, and slick lower back the unruly hairs to his satisfaction.

As it turns out, this gent once had a panel interview that day with 4-5 executives. And yes, the whole interview group was sitting in the conference room observing in disgust as this candidate groomed himself up shut and personal in genuine hillbilly fashion.

How would you manage a company handshake in this situation? Talk about a lack of interview etiquette!

11. Arrive 15 minutes early but no sooner

You are in no way permitted to be late for your interview; however, did you understand that arriving too early should be traumatic to employers? Find out why in this brief article I wrote on every other one of my webpages.

12. Promptly send a thank you be aware after your interview

This is imperative on your job interview custom list. This is not only common courtesy, but it also keeps your title in front of these who interviewed you.

If you comply with the tips outlined in this guide, you will find that you are successful in your job interview. Learning as tons as you are in a position related to the special sorts of interviews, as well as the organization, is relatively beneficial. Learning to reflect the personality of the interviewer, bringing alongside a portfolio, and asking your personal questions are all essential elements to creating a particular relationship with a company.

CHAPTER FIVE

Resume Writing - No work experience? No problem.

Everything occurs for the first time. First step. First kiss. First job hunts and finally, the first job resumes that we're going to talk about in this chapter. There is nothing weird that your palms begin shivering and sweating when it comes to writing your first resume, mainly if you suppose that you have no applicable ride or presentation skills.

Luckily, there is a way that proved you don't, in reality, want the transferable abilities or first-rate working history to get a job. The elaborate secret lies in the capability to show all your skills and achievements innovatively.

Wondering how to make your resume with no work experience the winner amongst others? Take a step and preserve scrolling. We'll go through this together step by step. No guarantees that it will be quick and easy, however in the end, you'll get a perfect resume with no job ride for sure.

1. Include a summary statement

Resume goal statements, the place you can kingdom exactly what career goals you desire to achieve, have generally fallen out of fashion. This is because you desire to focus on what you can do for the employer, no longer what the corporation can do for you. A resume precise statement, on the different hand, sums up who you are professionally at the top of the resume in a sentence or two and serves as the first impact you give a hiring supervisor to entice them to hold reading.

2. Decide on a resume format

There are some dominant resume templates in use today: functional, chronological, and hybrid, which is an aggregate of the two. A chronological resume layout lists a candidate's work journey in reverse-chronological order. A functional resume layout focuses on highlighting the candidate's skills and achievements as an alternative than work experience. While the functional resume structure can be a beautiful alternative for job seekers with little knowledge, most employers decide upon a chronological or hybrid resume format. Whatever resume layout you figure out to use, be sure that your structure stays regular at some stage in the document.

3. Pay attention to technical details

When enhancing your resume, make sure there is no punctuation, grammatical, spelling, or any mistakes that will make your resume look unprofessional. Then, have a friend, spouse, sibling or a stranger examine it once more to capture any errors you may have neglected — you cannot manage to pay for a typo or missing word. Also, be positive to fluctuate your language and utilize action verbs at some point in your resume to preserve your reader engaged.

4. Take stock of your achievements and activities

Make a list of the total achievement and jobs you've executed successfully that may be useful on a resume. From this list, you may then want to trim down what to include on your resume. Different things might be applicable to unique jobs you apply for, so hold a full list and pick out the most appropriate things from it to include on your resume when you send it out.

5. Focus on your education and skills

In lieu of work experience, it is great to increase and focus on your education and capabilities you've developed on your resume. What can you possibly offer that this job requires? What will be beneficial to the hiring company? What have you accomplished in college, and what have you studied that has prepared you for assuming this job? This is typically a little simpler if you're a college graduate with specialized education, but even a high school graduate can speak about their electives, why they wanted to take them, and what they realized from the class.

6. Internships, internships, internships

Unpaid and paid college internships are one of the fantastic weapons you have in opposition to "experienced level." In addition to the fact that they give you some certifiable work understanding, but they also permit you to network and make connections that can put you in a job later. When applying for a job besides experience, be favorable to listing any internships you completed. If you have not had one, consider making use of as a step earlier than an entry-level job.

7. Include any extracurricular activities or volunteer work

Whenever studied, most managers state that they mull over a volunteer outing close by paid work understanding. So, any humanitarian effort that features your abilities or where you realized a new ability you can put on your resume. It only consists of interests if they are relevant to the position and have equipped you with transferable skills that would be useful for the job role.

8. Never consist of these positive elements

While there are many factors you reflect on consideration on adding to your resume, there are a few matters you ought to by no means consist of on your resume due to the fact they waste space, don't inform the business enterprise whatever relevant, or may want to damage your brand. This list includes, however, is no longer limited, to references, writing samples, and photos of yourself. Do no longer add this fact to your resume, except a business enterprise or recruiter asks you to grant them. Besides, make positive you are now not the use of an unprofessional e-mail address. "Younggee@email.com" can also have sounded superb when you had been younger, but it's now not the proper message to convey to prospective employers. It's convenient to create a free, professional-looking electronic mail address for your job-search activities with platforms like Gmail.

9. Keywords, keywords, keywords

Most employers use some structure of an applicant tracking system (ATS) to scan and sort resumes. This can also seem unfair; however, it is a fact of contemporary hiring. To combat this, you will prefer to come up with and include a listing of key phrases in your resume when making use of for any job. The right place to discover these key phrases is in the job advert itself, or in commercials for comparable jobs. One caveat: Don't use meaningless, demanding "buzzwords," such as "go-getter," "team player," and "detail-oriented." Unfortunately, every now and then these keywords are the main keywords highlighted in the advertisement. If that is the case, you'll have to sneak them in alongside your designated accomplishments.

10. Add a cover letter

Even if one is now not required, it's commonly an excellent notion to send a short cowl letter along with your resume. Cover letters are the place your persona comes out, and you need to use them to make a case for why you are the ideal candidate for this job. A standout cover letter can convince a corporation to deliver you in for an interview, even if your resume doesn't have all the matters they'd like to see.

11. Customize your resume for each job you follow

The last and most important factor to take into account when developing a precise resume is to create it for every job to which you apply. Different job postings are going to have distinct keywords, exclusive job obligations listed, and so on. Appealing to each character employer's wants and job necessities is the best strategy for getting your application noticed.

In the end, there are no magical components for how to write a winning resume — the impeccable resume is the one that lands you the job. Be prepared to update and tweak your resume, even when you are easily employed. Use a hybrid resume format and focus on your abilities and training when you do not have any work journey to show. You'll eventually get that job — and achieve that much-coveted experience.

A Tale of Two Resumes: To Upgrade or to Update, What Is Your Finest Solution?

Often, I hear humans say, "I want to replace my resume." This usually pertains to embarking on a job search and capability adding new job associated statistics got from their last job hunt. Now different individuals, data technological know-how employees or otherwise, take one of a kind approaches and decide to upgrade their resume which usually involves a revision of massive portions to mirror their dreams and career increase from most cautiously and completely possible. Furthermore, an improvement can be better targeted to a specific opportunity, which is the place it can have great value right here I will quickly discuss the two resume strategies, their professionals and cons, and what may additionally be a pleasant answer for you.

Now before identifying which way to go, it is vital to take into account that a resume is one of the documents you will ever own, so making your high-quality presentation feasible is essential for your career fortunes.

In the hundreds, and on occasion thousands of resumes I see in a year, I would say the majority are resume updates. They consist of the whole of inserting or tacking on, their current, or last, job into the present structure of the resume they used in their previous search. This is a fundamental update, and regularly the least helpful. The next kind of update might also contain altering other components of your resume other than merely "tacking on" your ultimate job. Here we can also possibly see additions to your competencies or job description from your current job, and possibly, however least likely, going lower back to previous jobs to highlight those responsibilities that are most applicable to your cutting-edge job.

I find if any individual tacks on their current job to replace their resume, then the resume may also seem to be like the author both has little or no knowledge, or interest, in excessive-quality of resume construction. Worse, this may also give the influence that one is now not serious about a job search or is disorganized or not detail-oriented.

Indications of this may additionally be that the resume may additionally provide as much, or occasionally, even more, area to jobs that were from five, ten, or even fifteen plus years in the past than they a give to their current position. Now, on occasion, one would possibly be compelled to update their resume for an unforeseen, immediately want for a resume, by a recruiter...but face up to this urge for a quick fix as tons as possible.

Recently I obtained an example of such a replace from a Network Engineer with splendid competencies and stable work background. He had had one position for six years and then another job for six months, and he gave half as a good deal house to this truly outdated, from a technical perspective, prior position. Also, he described his modern-day job in the first person, which is usually now not regarded the quality approach, while his earlier positions have been described either in first or third, personal references. These inconsistencies detracted appreciably from what would be an ideal job candidate. It was apparent he, simple terms, his modern-day role barring plenty notion of how this would possibly appear to a resume screener.

In the above-stated instance a more cautiously regarded upgrade would offer extra complete description of their modern role which did not have that hasty "tacked-on look", also in updating the competencies and the summary, and editing the previous job description, my patron would want to change the preceding job descriptions reflect the contemporary position and future interests. One issue I saw in this resume and frequently in different updates is that the stressful of the verbs in the previous jobs want to be modified from the current anxious to the last annoying (e.g., from "is responsible" to "was responsible"). Luckily, in this case, as the 1/3 birthday party recruiter, I corrected all of these resume deficiencies, but frequently someone goes without delay to the corporation with a quick replace they, unfortunately, suppose true enough.

In a great update or upgrade, whether it is for a secretary, software engineer, or CEO, the length is usually a necessary consideration. Updates seldom tackle this issue; a top improve must! The content and structure of the first page are most important, although two, and from time to time more, pages are applicable to consist of all of your jobs. Here is the place you have the greatest possibility to attract, or repel, the hiring source. Skills, summaries, competencies, widespread accomplishments, all need to be shortly reachable here on the first page. Whether your resume is scanned by using software or hiring authority, relevant ability placement and volume can decide if your resume is acted on or discarded.

Also, in a desirable improve you must prune your previous job descriptions so that extra current jobs are given greater area and in the past positions show gradually less space. An accurate rule of thumb here is to strive to suppose like the hiring authority, and attempt to galvanize him or her with what you have done lately not doubtlessly lose their activity with overly verbose descriptions of what you did ten or twenty years ago. This matches the spacing strategy, and additionally, I would suggest concentrating on key elements of your background that, as much as possible, mainly relate to the jobs you are seeking. This might also sound tedious; however, it can supply you an incredible advantage over competing candidates who prefer an easy updating strategy. Recall, a resume is an advertisement for yourself, and the extra you can draw the hiring authorities to your message, the greater the likelihood they will buy!

For proper improvement, I would suggest you think about studying what the "best practices' in your industry, location of expertise, ride level. Susan Whitcomb's work "Resume Magic" and Martin Yate's "Knock em Dead" series offers outstanding upgrading or even rewriting, advice. Also, I recommend you particularly pay interest to codecs presented that fine visually symbolize your historical past and the role you are applying for. Again, Whitcomb and Yate provide brilliant recommendations and resume templates. What is essential is that the format, in particular, if you add graphics, does not distract, and with a bit of luck enhances the effectiveness of your resume. In my upgrade example, the candidate paid nearly no attention to critical layout issues, font selection, white space, or the benefits of using a more contemporary bullet format versus large blocks of text.

Now there are some occasions where you may additionally want to do a total rewrite like if you are thinking about altering careers or you are from any other country, like India, which has extraordinary resume standards. However, in these instances, there are typical "chunks" of job descriptions you can transpose from the old resume to the new. Also, some of us are not capable of putting an appealing resume collectively, even though we can also excel at what we do. In these cases, I recommend that you discover a specially rated resume writing service. For a few hundred bucks, this may be your solution. However, earlier than you hire a provider ask them to exhibit you a few samples of their work that relate at once to your history and aspirations.

Lastly, you must put a lot of concept into what your resume says about you and your background. Generally, this can also be all the viewpoints. The company may also know about you, specifically in this age of online resume submission. In most instances, I prefer an improvement over an update, with an entire rewrite to be regarded solely as a final resort. An update can seem "tacky," or tacked on until the preceding iterations of your resume are very well crafted and are cohesive and like-minded with the constrained new information you add. However, even then, the pruning procedure that is a hallmark of enhancements wishes to be considered. Upgrades have greater strategic cost than updates due to the fact you are more probable to look at your resume as complete.You may also see it as fits into your whole job search strategy. I know it is tempting to get a quick restore that some updates provide. However, prudence and persistence are essential in writing a job triumphing resume.

Resume Writers - How are you going to work with Them

More and more candidates are turning to professional resume writers to acquire a competitive facet in today's race for interviews and job offers. This area offers hints on how to get the most out of working with a professional resume writer. It's designed to assist all people who are thinking about shelling out giant dollars for a custom resume. Here are six suggestions:

Write your resume first with a free online resume constructing tool. I'll refer to one later.

Be engaged, listen and monitor how the report is progressing.

Take heed.

Ask questions.

Be responsive.

Understand your resume writer.

OK, let's say you see a job you are perfect for. Or possibly you simply bought a "layoff" be aware of the job you've had for ten years. You will do good for yourself to aim for that perfect job, or you're geared up to launch into a robust job hunt. There's no doubt that the first question the organization will say is, "Send me your resume." So, you ask yourself, "What's the excellent way to go about getting a good resume?"

1. Write your very own - You're probable amazed to see that my first tip is to attempt to write your very own resume first. Yes, that is right. I motivate everybody to at least supply it a try. It's a no-lose situation. Here are two motives why:

You just may additionally have what it takes to profile your value to a prospective employer. You can nicely format a document; outline your skills, abilities, trip, and credentials genuinely and succinctly. You know the correct length and how to bundle and send it. And it saves you money. Bingo!

Or, let's say you've got spent hours writing, struggling, attempting to discern out what you are going to put in and what to leave out, how to section it correctly, the place and what to name skills, abilities, core values. The punctuation is iffy, and your sentence structure is questionable. You've given it a try; however, you realize the writing might not stand up to the withering scrutiny of a resume review. So what have you gained? Simply put, higher information about who you are and what is your value. Call it research.

You are more engaged in the system due to the fact you wrote the basics. You know more about yourself than you did earlier before you commenced the process. You're prepared to hand over the important points to an expert resume creator and discuss the details. You're organized to sit in the front of an interview committee and protect your resume because you were a significant section of the process. And when they ask if you wrote the resume yourself, you can efficiently say,

"Yes." You can say you employed a professional resume marketing consultant to edit it.

Let's face it; it is no longer easy, writing about yourself. So you engage with a writer. S/he doesn't comprehend you, barring for what's been stated in your preliminary meeting, and perhaps what's in the resume you've given her. From this factor on, realize your author can solely do so much besides your help. They will try it. They will do the whole lot they can. But it relies upon you to permit them to make it the first-class resume possible. You've located a Professional Resume Writer. Take note:

2. Engage Completely- The unengaged purchaser is probably the toughest component for a resume writer to deal with. Just because you've paid a writer does not imply, the writer would comprehend what to write. The writer is not a clairvoyant. The measure of a precise resume creator is to ask probing questions. We writers ask for facts in many methods about many elements and topics of who you are. It would possibly seem that what we ask has little relevance. But crafting price statements, profile summaries, skills, abilities, experience and core values is like painting a portrait. It takes a range of hues on a pallet to combine into just the right shade, hue and spotlight for a gorgeous image of who you are. You can say a resume is much the same. Listen, listen, hear cautiously and give carefully measured responses.

3. Take Heed- The excellent writers know what sells. Even though all resume writers are different, there are frequent denominators contained in all excellent resumes. "Write in the lively voice, shorter is better, simple formatting, listing accomplishments, scale back out fluff and redundancies." Just to identify a few. This isn't to say that they shouldn't apprehend it's your resume and you have to experience blissful with it. What I'm saying is that the resume creator doesn't normally know what works you are applying for. By offhandedly denying them their writing instincts only complicates their work and makes it difficult for them to be aware of what to do.

4. Ask Questions- If it doesn't appear right, ask questions. Professional resume writers would love you to ask and support them throughout the process. It's a collaborative process, and they desire you engaged. My clients must be contented with my final delivery. After all, they will have to defend it at some point in an interview. If I do not get questions, I tend to surprise if I'm hitting the mark for the client. And when the final resume is submitted, and the task is closed, so to speak, it is awkward to get a telephone call a week later with two or three items that have been discussed during the unique process.

5. Be Responsive- The resume writing technique commonly is a back-and-forth modifying process. When purchasers ask me how long it takes to write their resume, I say, "It depends on the client." Best resumes come from the writer and the consumer being carefully engaged for a quick, targeted time. Considerable lapsed time with the aid of the customer to respond to a request for data or clarification by the author - usually more than 2 or 3 days - gives way to diminishing focus, alternatively slight it may be. And when the center of attention is lost, so erodes some of the class of the process.

6. Other Clients- high-quality resume writers are busy. They may additionally average as many as 5 to ten purchasers a month. As lots as right writers prefer to make you sense like you're the sole customer they have, be aware of they have others they are working with at the equal time. Honor your scheduled instances for phone calls, evaluation discussions, meetings, etc. Make yourself on hand and submit your questions in a bunch, alternatively than three or four calls in a day with a one-of-a-kind query or advice on each call. Those are some of the things that will come out of attempting to write your professional resume first. Organization. So, do your homework. Make sure you try your hand at writing your very own resume first. If it is going to take a pro to assist you, so be it. In most instances, you will be comfortable with the end result if you are well involved in the procedure yourself.

CHAPTER SIX

How to Prepare for Job Interviews

If you are invited for a job interview, this potential, the attainable organization has examined your resume and determined you may be the right person for the job. So, as soon as you get this far, you're already an exact phase of the way there.

These are some pointers on how to ace the interview and land the job.

Research the company: My research over and over indicates that employers and hiring managers desire candidates to look up the company before the interview and that most candidates no longer do this. Do your lookup, and you appreciably make bigger your hazard of getting hired. This potential understanding of what the organization does and the small print of the jobs for which you're applying. Some other matters you can attempt to discover out include:

The company's mission and values

What the organization lifestyle is like

Who their administration team is?

Who their competition is?

Who their clients are?

How they attain their market

Some ways to discover this out include:

The company website

Company social media accounts

Glassdoor – this is a web page that compiles worker critiques of and different information about the organizations. (https://www.glassdoor.ca/index.htm)

Corporate blog

The news

Dress professionally and be appropriately groomed. Dressing professionally may suggest exclusive things in one of a kind industry. If you're not sure, it's exceptional to err on the side of formality and put on a suit or a conservative outfit. Make sure you're easy and neat. Some would possibly suppose this advice is apparent; however, we understand that now, not all people can pay interest to it. Make positive your breath is fresh!

Brush your enamel, and don't overdose on cologne or perfume. And don't smoke beforehand.

Be on schedule or somewhat early. Try not to be late for the prospective employee meet-up. Try not to be too soon, either. Five or ten minutes ahead of schedule is fine. Ensure you know precisely where you're going so you don't get missing on the way (and wind up being late).

Bring a replica of your resume. Bring a printed copy of your resume and of any different archives that may be required.

Be friendly to all the people you meet. Be pleasant to everyone, including the security personnel, the receptionist, and the character who lets the door shut in your face while you're entering the building. You in no way understand who is looking at or who knows who – the man you snap at due to the fact he's in your way may be the man you're interviewing with. Also, it's just necessary to be professional and kind.

Offer a firm handshake. Don't supply a limp handshake or hold close someone's hand to the extent that you will harm them if they have arthritis or whitlow. Be firm and confident.

Smile and make eye contact. Smile! You want to convey that you are pleasant and likable. Making eye contact suggests that you are fascinated and alert. Don't stare into the person's eyes. Just make positive about maintaining eye contact.

Get ready to **answer the following questions.** On an occasion that you are a newcomer, you might be requested some one-of-a-kind questions from what is always asked in job interviews – about your language skills, perhaps, or about your traveling experience. Here, however, are some of the questions most frequently asked in job interviews.

Tell me about your self – Just about every job interview begins with a model of this question. Don't talk about how much you love cats (unless you're applying for a job at a veterinarian clinic). Talk about how your professional pursuits make you the right candidate for the role.

What makes you fascinated in this job? – Don't say you want the money. Employers are extra impressed with candidates who are passionate about working for them, mainly than with any individual who is just looking for a new gig. Explain what you assume is fantastic about the organization or the role, and how the job excites you.

What do you know about our company? – Again, organizations opt for candidates who prefer to work for them, so they appear for candidates who have executed their research. Channel your conversation to the company's mission, services or products, brand, and how you'd intend to contribute.

What would you say your most significant strengths are? – This looks like a convenient query – are you aware of what you're properly good at? However, don't take this question strictly at face value. Read the job description carefully and describe a capability of yours that would lend itself to being particularly successful on the job. Just make certain that they're proper strengths. You don't need to declare to be good at something you don't without a doubt understand how to do.

What do you suppose are your biggest weaknesses? – It looks like a trick. If you answer fairly, you're acknowledging to something that could probably turn off an employer. If you say "I have no weaknesses. I am flawless," the company will identify you definitely lack in self-awareness or either a liar. You have to say something. Think of a true weakness, something that isn't important requirement for the job, and give an explanation for how you became aware of it and are working on improving upon it. This indicates that you are reflective, inclined to strive and to learn to get better. Try not to say you're a perfectionist or a workaholic. Everyone says that.

Tell me about a challenging state of affairs you encountered at work and how you handled it? – It's effortless to appear advantageous and assured when the whole thing is going well. With this question, the company desires to comprehend how you measure up when things get challenging. Talk about setback at work or conflict, how you dealt with it professionally, and what you realized from it.

Where do you see yourself in a few years? – Depending on the position and the level of the job, you don't have to pretend that you choose to still be in it in 5 years. Most people intend to grow in their careers, and five years has become a long time to remain in one position. Instead, explain how the job is the proper move for your profession boom at this moment – and how your excelling at it would make each you and the agency more successful. Show how what you can accomplish, exhibit and study in this job takes you nearer to where you desire to go.

Why should we employ you? – This is a handy one. It's no longer a trick question – employers are offering you the hazard to sell yourself. Simply explain why you are enthusiastic about the job and how the accomplishments you've executed in the past exhibit your capability to be brilliant at it. Be confident, but now not cocky. Don't say, "Because I need the job."

Do you have any questions for me? – This is your risk to take manipulate of the interview. You can frequently carry your competence and self-belief to a business enterprise more impressively with the questions you are going to ask than the ones you answer. Asking intelligent questions can demonstrate that you have some know-how of the industry and that you're already thinking about how you can make contributions to it. Do not say, "No." Also, do not ask questions like, "what is the pay?"; "when am I entitled for a vacation?"; or "how long does it normally take to become promoted?"

Plan stories. For a portion of the above inquiries, you should have a story prepared, for example, one about a period you managed a difficult situation. Make sure you have these testimonies organized, so you don't get stuck with anything to say.

Get the electronic mail addresses of everybody you interview with. If you are able, gain contact details for every person you meet with.

Follow up with a thank-you note. Send a thank-you to observe afterward, later that equal day. Thank the humans who met with you for taking the time to meet with you, and reiterate your pastime in the position and why you are awesomely healthy for the activity and the position. Keep it short.

At that point, you pause. If there is no feedback for possibly 14 days, follow up again in an email. Keep that observe-up short as well. Just say you have been without a doubt excited about the job and are hoping that there has been some development. Then depart it. Many employers are very impolite and will not let you recognize that you didn't get the job. You will never hear from them again. If three weeks pass, you can likely expect this is the case. Move on and preserve making use of until you are hired.

If you cannot get the first few jobs, don't get discouraged. Everyone gets rejected, and it's usually painful. Eventually, any person will say "Yes! You are exactly what I need!"

Job Interviewing - Do's and Don'ts - Before, During and After the Interview

Nearly all job seekers are familiar with the importance of getting ready for a job interview. That skill is more than simply brandishing your resume with a smile on your face. You are most likely to understand at least some of the matters you do to get ready. However, have you additionally notion about what you no longer do - before, in the course of and after an interview? We've noted a "Top 10-12" list of Do's and Don'ts for the before and after of any job interview. Follow these, and you can be assured you will be ready to make a success of that interview - and confidently and rapidly pass to the top of the Hiring Manager's "hiring" list.

Before the job interview - earlier than you arrive at the enterprise

Do research the agency (and the interviewers, if possible) to study as lots as you can. Don't act cocky all through the interview to show off your research

Do realize that there are unique sorts of job interviews and discover out which kind you will be having. Don't walk into a surprise!

Do assessment feasible interview questions and put together your responses. Don't memorize your answers or over-rehearse so you may not sound rehearsed at the interview.

Do role-play if possible with a friend or family member and ask for comments on your presentation. Don't ask anybody who cannot be objective, however.

Do take an exercise run to the interview region to be positive you comprehend exactly where it is and how long it may also take you to arrive. Don't get lost (and if for some loopy reason you do get misplaced on the way, don't say that to the interviewer).

Do layout to arrive 5-10 minutes early. Don't arrive any earlier or you might also appear desperate. And if you are running late, Do name the interviewer or different organization representative to let them know your expected arrival time.

Do recognize that your interview begins way earlier than you greet the interviewer(s). It really begins the moment you start the day trip to that interview. Be alert and courteous at all times. You never be aware of who you can also interact with as you head to the interview. Don't lose your cool. Be alert and courteous to everyone!

Do ask for the organization's dress code. Don't count on you automatically recognize even if the business enterprise is comparable to a preceding employer.

Focus on your oral hygiene and speaking manner. Brush your teeth before the interview. Use a breath mint or mouthwash. Don't smoke earlier than - or for the duration of - the interview, even if the interviewer smokes and offers a cigarette, etc.

Switched off your cell phone or pager (or put it in silent vibration) and don't turn it returned on until the interview is completed.

During the interview - from the inception to the time you leave

Do greet the receptionist with respect. Here is a place where you can make a fantastic first impression. Don't anticipate they won't be requested for their input after you leave.

Do whole a job software without comment, if you are given one. Don't draw back and say your resume has everything on it.

Do bring additional resumes and or job abilities "sales brochures" and provide to all interviewers. Don't anticipate anybody to have a copy already.

Do greet the interviewer(s) through title; e.g., Mr., Mrs., Ms., Dr., and remaining name. Don't count on you understand the pronunciation of the last name. If the least unsure, ask the receptionist earlier than going into the interview.

Do shake palms with absolutely everyone who affords their hand. Shake their hand firmly. Don't have a clammy or limp handshake, and wait until you are supplied a seat before sitting down. And take note that physique language regularly speaks louder than words. Sit properly, be attentive and show interest at all times. Make top eye contact with the interview. Don't slouch, fidget, turn out to be distracted or stare at the interviewer.

Do display enthusiasm for the employer and job; and a high stage of strength and confidence. Don't be soft-spoken, overly assertive or show up anxious or desperate to get the job (or simply any job just to be employed), however.

Do you sell yourself? Make positive that your accomplishments come throughout to the interviewer(s) in a way that genuinely speaks at once to their company's needs. Show how you can benefit their company. Don't anticipate your software or resume to do the sales job for you, and do not provide any terrible facts about yourself.

Do take gain of your time with the interviewer to evaluate them and their enterprise as an achievable employer and your mutual "fit." Don't neglect a chance to ask questions as you might also appear as although you are no longer interested.

Do reply to questions completely. Answer confidently and succinctly but no "yes" or "no" answers. Offer examples, explanations; exhibit your talents, skills, and accomplishments. Don't over-answer, however. Know when to stop.

Be ready for the surprising questions. To give your self-time to think, repeat the query or ask the interviewer to repeat it. A brief 1-2 seconds pause is OK. Don't, however, make uncomfortable pauses, or statements such as, "Wow, it is a suitable one!" which make you appear unprepared.

Do attempt to lengthen any dialogue about salary, vacations, bonuses, etc., till after you have an offer. Be prepared for a question about your income and ensure you give a natural response. If you comprehend the revenue vary the company is imparting, and it is suited to you say, "I'm sure we can locate agreement inside your profits range." Don't provoke the discussion.

Do always act as if you have decided not to get the job. In no way must you close the door on the probability that you might be employed by the company until you are sure; When you behave rudely, the job is no longer for you. Try not to mess yourself up on the off chance that you desire the chance by bringing up non-public issues, controversial topics, something bad about former colleagues and employers, telling jokes, the use of terrible language, chewing gum

Do close the interview by expressing your hobby in the job. Ask what the subsequent steps are, and when the employer will make a hiring decision. Do ask for business cards from every man or woman you interviewed with. Don't make assumptions about even easy names; get the spelling on the off chance that you were unable to get the card.

Do catch the highpoints of the interview immediately after. Don't overlook the necessary details.

Do have a motion design in location-based totally on a strong, well-thought-out interview follow-up strategy. This can provide you with a massive aggressive advantage over others who interviewed for the job and do not follow-up. Don't let this be a haphazard pastime with no structure; simply a letter here, a call there. There's no higher way to lose a probability than to supply little follow-up importance.

Do write thank you letters within 24 hours to every individual who interviewed you to continue to exhibit your pastime and enthusiasm for the corporation and job, except sounding desperate. Don't fail to ship a thank you, even if the job doesn't suit you and way below your skills and certification.

Do focus on the content of the thank you letters, no longer so an awful lot on whether it is hand-written or typed. Show appreciation for the company's activity in you and remind those receiving a thank you letter why you are the uniquely certified candidate for the position. Don't ship the thank you letter via the flawed medium, however; make certain you know the first-class way to attain those interviewers - normal mail, email, fax, a phone call., etc. And do not have any mistakes in your thank you notes.

Do alert your references, if you have not already, that they might also acquire a name from your potential employer. Don't forget about to brief them on what was once stated - by way of you and the interviewers - at some stage in the interview.

Ensure to follow-up, especially if requested by the interviewer(s). Don't go overboard, however. Do be patient. You must work with the company's timeline. Don't, however, end your job search - even if you're confident you may get the job. Continue to are seeking out other possibilities and interviews. This can be of advantage to you in 2 ways: a. In the event you secure the job, you can leverage different gives in your job offer negotiations b. Should you not get the job, you may have other possibilities to pursue.

Do flip a terrible scenario (not getting the job) into a superb (getting a referral). Add the questioners to your pursuit of employment organize. Support this maturing relationship with the goal that you can request that they allude you to different contacts. Don't, in different words, ever burn any of the bridges you construct in your job search. Always suppose of approaches to utilize them - and to respond. Doing so can profit you now and later on - for some other quest for new employment wishes as well as developing your career.

There you have it, and the pinnacle Do's and Don'ts for acing your interview.

The job advertisement is a consistently evolving aspect of job recruitment. In some cases, it supports the job searcher by offering them the opportunity to see a shortage of ability. In any case, today it is the hiring associations that hold the high ground. There is an abundance of qualified people for most job openings. So on the off chance that you have been effective in increasing an interview you should have the option to make the best of the chance and convert it to a job offer. Figuring out how to prepare for an interview will give you an aggressive edge. Sadly, the vast majority don't invest a lot of energy into interview planning. They appear and trust in the best. On the off chance that you come steadily, you will stand out in the hiring mind when competitor's qualities and shortcomings are considered.

Center your arrangement in the accompanying four territories:

Research the company and the position.

Start by visiting the company site. You can learn a great deal about their needs and current methodologies. In any case, don't stop here, you have to encourage your research by researching flow news things about the company. This will once in a while reveal important data that will exhibit your genius. If conceivable, chat with current/previous employees to study the association's way of life. By researching various sources you get a progressively complete image of the company.

Prepare your outcomes situated stories.

A hiring chief is attempting to decide whether you are an ideal choice for the position. The goal isn't to determine if you are a decent individual, however on the off chance that you have the capability and experience to increase the value of the association. As you prepare for the interview, you have to make results situated examples of overcoming adversity that you can tell during the interview. These victories will exhibit your gifts and capacity to accomplish results. An example of overcoming adversity ought to contain three components; *1) portray the circumstance, 2) depict what you did, and 3) recognize the particular results accomplished.* You are situating yourself as the perfect individual for the job.

Prepare answers to normal questions.

Most hiring supervisors won't set aside the effort to think about innovative questions to ask during an interview. They will ask the normal interview questions, for example, "tell about yourself", and so forth. There are numerous productions you can acquire that will cover the many interview questions that can be asked. The important point is that you should be prepared to answer these types of questions in a presented and all around considered way. Showing trust in your answers will help persuade the hiring administrator of your capacities to take care of business.

The main part of the questions you are asked will originate from your resume. Survey your resume and foresee questions that may be asked by the interviewer. For instance, you might be asked to clarify how you moved toward a particular achievement recorded by one of your previous jobs. This is an extraordinary chance to relate an outcomes arranged story you have just prepared. Numerous questions will occur by what's not explicitly expressed on a resume, for example holes in business, horizontal job changes, random jobs. By planning ahead of time you can answer such that will evacuate any worries that might be waiting

Prepare Questions to Ask

This is a territory that is commonly neglected by those in anticipation of an interview. This is a point at which you can separate yourself from the challenge. These are questions about the company, its items/benefits, its systems, target clients and job obligations to give some examples. They are not questions about advantages, pay, or excursion time. You ask these questions to pass on understanding and information that others won't try to illustrate. You can ask driving questions that will enable you to recount an example of overcoming adversity that exemplifies the value you can bring to the company. By asking intriguing questions you will have some authority over the heading of the interview. I have been surprised at the high level of individuals I have interviewed people who asked no creative or imaginative questions. It makes one marvel now a lot of intrigue and excitement they will bring to the job whenever procured.

If you truly center around these four territories in how to prepare for an Interview you will be miles in front of your opposition. Your additional exertion will be noted and could be the distinction in a job offer or a dismissal letter.

Imprint Gregory, outcomes arranged official with 34 years of involvement with secretly held and Fortune 1000 companies, is the creator of the recently made 'The How to Prepare for an Interview' blog. His experience incorporates making a provincial hiring plan which brought about the hiring of 100 deals and deals bolster people in a month's time. As a major aspect of the arrangement, he built up the hiring profiles for the situations to be filled, made the up-and-comer screening process and prepared the hiring directors in an appropriate interview procedure. He will share his involvement with what hiring administrators search for in an applicant, traps to stay away from, and how to situate yourself as an alluring employee.

At the point when an employer chooses to lead an interview with you, there are sure things that they are searching for from you. Usually, you are probably going to concentrate on these things during an interview. However, you ought to recall the entirety of the tips in this manual since following those tips is what is going to make the employers see those things in you.

Since everyone needs to have an advantage with regards to an interview, it normally appeared to be suitable to give you access to what the employers are assessing you on during an interview. So here is that rundown.

Your Enthusiasm: Employers need to realize that you are willing and anxious to be a piece of their company. Being completely armed with information about the company is a sure way and good approach to show your energy and readiness.

Your capacity to talk obviously: If you approach an interview murmuring and talking slang, a forthcoming employer won't consider you to be an expert.

Demonstrating your cooperation aptitudes: You should show a case of your capacity to function as a group during your interview.

Leadership aptitudes: You should show your leadership capacities by moving toward your interview with a hostile line of reasoning.

Critical thinking capacity: Employers have to realize that you can deal with yourself when an issue shows up.

Business-related experience: You certainly need to show that you have some involvement with the field as of now, so the employer realizes that you won't be overpowered.

Network inclusion: Employers love to see that you have done some humanitarian works. It shows that you invest heavily in your locale, and an eagerness to be a cooperative

Company information: Again, this stipulates employers like to see that you have done your research about their company. It shows that your enthusiasm for working for the company is unrivaled.

Adaptability: Employers need to realize that you can take the path of least resistance. It demonstrates that they can rely upon you later.

Desire and Motivation: Ambitious individuals are commonly persuaded enough to make extraordinary upgrades in the company as they are walking their way up the ladder. Aspiration generally implies more cash for the company.

Relationship building abilities: Your capacity to coexist with others is important to an employer. They have to realize that you won't cause some disruption you are procured.

Proficient appearance: Nobody needs a good-for-nothing working in their office. Be sure to dress fittingly for the job that you are applying for.

Capacity to Multitask: This is getting the chance to be an essential staff in the work environment. Most days, you will be asked to multitask. Regardless of whether you are not, employers need to realize that you can do it without going nuts on them.

PC Ease: These days, pretty much every company on the planet is running on PCs. The capacity to work a PC with at any rate negligible measure of straightforwardness is essential. It is ideal for keeping a decisive advantage over the most popular programming like MS Office, Quark Express, and Linux.

Reliability: Employers need trustworthy and principled individuals to work for them. Your ability to keep to time and to arrive at an agreed place on time is a good place to begin when attempting to demonstrate that you have good qualities.

CHAPTER SEVEN

15 Most Frequent Interview Questions (and how to respond to them)

How to get employed through nailing the 15 most common interview questions employers ask. From obvious questions such as 'why do you desire to work for us?' to weird and wacky ones like 'if you had been an animal what would you be?', you'll have a head start with the fantastic answers. Read our pointers from top interview professionals and be higher prepared at your interview than everybody else.

You've landed a job interview. Congratulations!

And now you're studying this guide, which capacity you recognize getting ready interview solutions is key to getting the job.

You're already above some of your competition.

Prepared candidates supply detailed, concise and applicable answers, which is what employers prefer to hear.

Through preparation ability, you'll be more confident, less anxious of the unknown and a good deal much less probable to go through from interview nerves.

If you're getting ready for an interview, we have some proper news:

To help you with the interview, I have highlighted some of the most common interview questions. For every frequent interview question, these specialists also inform us:

What the corporation wishes to know. By employer, we suggest the interviewer(s) and hiring manager(s).

How to respond to the interview question

How not to reply to the question.

The conventional approaches interviewers phrase questions. We find the most frequent interview questions are often asked in barely distinctive ways.

Before getting into the specifics of the 15 questions, it's well worth drawing your attention to two killer pieces of interview advice that experts agree to apply to all interview questions:

First, healthy your skills, competencies and experiences with those the agency requested in their job advert.

Second, come up with your very own answers to these common questions. Don't give stock replies. You won't locate equipped made solutions here. Instead, we'll help you supply your real quality answer.

1. Tell me about yourself

What is the company expecting from you? This is likely the most frequent interview question. It's regularly the first to be asked and, due to the fact it's an open question, it's a hard one to answer.

A company will have developed an effect on you from your CV and cowl letter. Your reply to this question shortly helps them decide the accuracy of that impression. It additionally gives them a probability to have a look at your ranges of self-assurance and composure, via your voice and physique language.

How to answer

Answer this query in phrases of the competencies and experience required for the position. Start with a short precis of your career history. Then provide them with a brief overview of how your profession has developed, focusing extra on what you've learned or achieved.

You might choose to prepare by way of writing down a few key factors, which you can rehearse before the interview.

To make sure you've given the business enterprise all the information they need, end your response by asking them if there's something they'd like you to give more detail.

Remember to task your voice, due to the fact it'll give the effect you're assured and composed.

How not to answer

Candidates often make the mistake of pronouncing a great deal when answering this question. Don't ramble, be brief. A one- to two-minute summary is the proper length.

There's no need to go into element at this early factor in the interview, as the agency will dig deeper into specifics later on. Repeatedly the major turn off in an applicant is when they say what they assume interviewers choose to hear and it just doesn't ring true.

Finally, as with all interview questions, don't supply a customary answer. Ensure your points are tailor-made to the position you're applying for.

2. What do you be aware of the organization?

What the corporation wishes to know

You can't comprehend the whole lot about a corporation from the outside, but it's essential to be aware of the basics.

We don't desire or anticipate a candidate to memorize reams of information from the website; however, we do count on them to have an understanding of who we are, what we do, our merchandise and services, and what they can do to enhance the company.

The organization will expect you to comprehend there:

Industry/sector.

Goals.

Key challenges.

Major competitors.

Culture and values.

They additionally wish to discover if you're enthusiastic about the prospect of working for them. Make positive you reveal your enthusiasm through your answer.

Researching each aspect of your job interview is crucial. Too frequently, I have had candidates who have claimed substantial ranges of enthusiasm for a role yet have no considerable knowledge of the business. If a candidate's knowledge extends little past the homepage of the employer's website, it suggests they can't sincerely be bothered.

The question regularly leads to 3 Why do you prefer to work for us?

How to answer

The key to a wonderful answer is thorough research.

It's necessary to do your research and make it clear you sincerely prefer to join this organization and no longer that this is one of 100 jobs you've utilized.

With these you can research any organization; they include:

The company's own website or careers website.

Job boards.

Press releases from the company or its competitors

Industry-specific publications to research greater about the sector

 But don't stop there. Researching about the company; its values, ambitions, and structure will show that you have thought about the move greater holistically.

Don't be afraid to get innovative in your research. For example, if you're going for an income assistant job at a retailer, visit one of its high street shops to get first-hand information on the role.

How not to answer

Don'repeat the contents of the business's website, or the enterprise description in the job advert.

3. Why do you intend working with us?

What the organization wants to know

The enterprise wants to uncover your motivations for the job.

Is it salary, location, brand, crew fit, or job title that is most important to you? This can range vastly between people. What might be an incredible brand for one character may no longer attraction to anybody else.

Employers additionally use this question to screen bogus candidates who've only applied because they want to take a look at the market or to negotiate a higher profit with their modern employer.

How to answer

To answer this question successfully, the center of attention on the employer's needs, not what you want.

It helps to demonstrate that you're an excellent suit for the role.

Show your knowledge of the enterprise by mentioning something unique about the job that really hobbies you.

It can be their new traces of business or technology they use – make positive you've achieved your research.

You could also discuss the organization's tradition or administration structure.

It's glaringly that once a candidate exhibits little interest in this question due to zero research or preparation, it shows they aren't prepared for the job and not the right candidate for the job. It's now not that we are self-important. We want humans who prefer to work with us, and candidates who want to have continually executed their homework.

Although your focal point is on the employer's needs, they might also ask you about your private motivations. One approach is to discuss your long-term profession potentialities with them.

If they deduce that you're not qualified, talk about the trials you can discover in the role. If they're deducing, you're underqualified, indicate that you can learn faster and that grow with them is one of your fundamental motivations.

How not to answer

A big mistake is to reply to this query by saying bad things about your present employer.

You can discuss looking progression, besides saying your boss is blocking off your growth at your modern company.

Don't body your reply in the past or present — instead, the focal point on the future.

This is no longer the time to deliver up revenue or benefits, or enormously minor incentives such as free parking space.

And keep away from sounding desperate for the job. Be clear that you don't just accept any job, but that you desire this job.

4. What can you deliver to the company?

What the organization wants to know

The enterprise wishes to examine your abilities with those required for the role.

They're additionally looking for your Unique Selling Proposition (USP).

It's a way of asking why they provide you with the job.

How to answer

Before the interview, learn about the job advert and determine out the employer's five most sought-after abilities and competencies.

Think deeply about your work history (and training if applicable). For each skill, come up with a short example that explains how you obtained or improved that knowledge, and how your possession of it benefited your agency at the time.

If you comprehend anyone who already works for the employer, ask them if they need a related talent or carrier that hasn't been noted in the job ad. If you can show interest in something they're searching for, your answer will be especially strong.

How you work

Your passion for the industry.

Your motivation to provide results.

Ways you can deliver a sparkling standpoint to the business.

Always ensure you tie these into the function you're applying for.

Don't fear if you can't fill each checkbox. The best candidate rarely exists, and interviewers and recruiters are properly aware of this.

It may also be that on paper, your experience is no longer right now relevant; however, the top candidates create angles that show you why all ride is the proper experience for the job.

How not to answer

Candidates frequently make the mistake of not the usage of examples to lower back up their answers.

Anyone can say that they have organizational skills, for example, but if you say something specific such as I have remarkable organizational skills. In the last 12 months, I have overseen 10 company occasions with up to 250 contestants each, and you are going to create a good impression.

This question is also phrased as

Why do you assume you're suitable for this role?

Why we ought to appoint you?

What would you bring to the team?

5. What are your weaknesses?

What the company is looking forA company will ask this to know if you're conscious of your weaknesses, and whether or not or now not you have strategies in the vicinity to tackle them.

We all have weaknesses. It is recognizing them that is significant. The questioner is searching for you to act naturally mindful. Getting ready for this inquiry can be extreme. Contemplate an appropriate shortcoming, and think of a sensible and practicable procedure for conquering it.

Some companies also use the question to see how you operate underneath pressure. It's as a lot about your physique language, as it is the answer.

How to answer

It can be hard to suppose of a weakness.

One trick is to ask your friends and family what professional qualities they would like you to work on. Even better, anybody at your current job who you trust completely. They're more likely to give applicable feedback. The obvious hazard is that your employer would possibly locate out you're looking for some other job.

Don't reference any faults that would directly weaken your capability to do the job. Talk about a part of improvement – something you're working on at the moment. For example, encompass sharpening up abilities in a precise area, such as taking an online course, or showing how you manipulate your studying agenda.

Describe your weakness.

Explain how you're working to overcome it.

Here are some things you should say:

Previously, when managing more than one tasks at the identical time, I wasn't in a position to prioritize and remember my work. To overcome this, each day, I created a prioritized to-do list.

I used to spend too plenty of time on tasks that weren't the best possible priority. Now I'm higher at allocating my time to things that supply cost to the business.

I used to get anxious giving presentations, so I enrolled in a course to enhance my public speaking.

Another tactic is to choose a weak spot that isn't imperative to the role, even though it's no longer integral to the role, you nonetheless want to make positive.

How not to answer

Don't select a weak point that's electricity in disguise. Interviewers go through your answer, and it'll appear as open-minded advice and thought. A classic, cliched instance is "I'm a perfectionist." Interviewees are often suggested to use it. Don't. The recommendation is outdated.

Don't highlight something that's a key talent for the job. Give some other example that isn't on the list of essentials.

And make sure you don't say that you don't have any weaknesses.

This question can also be phrased as

What is your greatest weakness?

Tell me about your weaknesses.

What are your strengths and weaknesses?

Tell me about your essential development areas.

What areas do you need to increase the most?

6. What are your strengths?

What the corporation desires to know

Employers are fascinated by how your skills, potential and experiences healthy what they need for the role. They choose to be aware of if you have the applicable abilities and journey for the job.

Perfect your answer to this question, and improve your probabilities of getting the job considerably.

Another way they would possibly ask the query is What can you deliver to the firm? (question four).

How To Reply

Go through the job advert and pick out the key competencies and competencies wished for the role. When researching the company, additionally hold a lookout for any information that shows what abilities and skills it's looking for.

Memorize five top competencies, the hiring manager will be searching for in their perfect candidate. Then work out how you can promote your transferable capabilities and experience.

Especially think about how your strengths could set you aside from others. Describe a strength, which you can demonstrate, is wished by using the role, and you will revel in using.

Make it clear how your present-day enterprise has benefited from your strengths.

How not to answer

You shouldn't list strengths that aren't relevant to the job you're making use of for. make sure you are not shy about your achievements.

The mistakes people make is to think of this as bragging. The first-rate element to do is to fit your pinnacle three strengths with what they're searching for – that's a good deal more effective.

You should keep away from common buzzwords and clichés. Phrases such as 'I work nicely independently as nicely as in a team.

Talk about the strengths that you'll bring to the role.

Most of all, don't be dishonest. It's no longer solely unethical; however, there's also a serious danger you'll get caught out.

This question is also be asked as follow:

What are the key strengths that you'll convey to this role?

What are your key skills?

7. Why is there a hole in your work history?

What the organization wants to know

To keep away from this question, don't leave a gap in your employment records on your job utility.

From your interviewer, a gap is a pink flag. It should put doubt in their mind when there is no need for none. You can counter this via having a real looking explanation for it.

The most frequent motives for a gap on the CV are:

Redundancy.

Dismissal.

Traveling/gap year.

Personal/health issues.

Is it a career.

It is a parent.

The enterprise will think about whether you put the time to exact. For example, did you apply for a course to improve your talent set, or tour to develop your horizons? Or, on the flip side, did you waste your time, via not actively job seeking.

How to answer

What you did all through the time you have been off.

Your track file in your previous jobs

If possible, discuss something optimistic you did all through your time off, like preparing for a necessary exam, volunteering or finishing an MBA. Mention capabilities or knowledge you cultivated during this time.

If you went traveling, inform us why you went, what you learned. Tell us how you use your time; was it spent productively?

If there's a vital role in your employment and you had been keeping it a private issue, you have all the right to say it.: I was once dealing with something non-public and decided to take a leave from the place of business to permit me to focus on getting that resolved as quickly as possible.

How not to answer

Don't say you've been doing nothing!

10. Tell me a fulfillment you are proud about

What the employer wishes to know

An agency asks this question to look out what you reflect on consideration as necessary, and what your priorities are.

As a business, you're not just recruiting any individual to do that role, and you're searching for a personality. You desire a rounded individual if anybody describes a venture that indicates resilience, such as finishing an enduring fitness challenge or a charitable accomplishment that shows a strong social and moral conscience.

How to reply

You can say something that speaks about your values. Organizing a fundraising or sports event, taking part in a race, or studying and the use of a new language or musical instrument are exact examples.

Again, strive to marry your selected achievement with capabilities and behaviors that are pertinent for the job. This is a terrific possibility to spotlight the strengths that you will convey to the function on your very own terms.

Work-based achievements are not often recognized with an award or celebration, so it's handy to lose tune of them or neglect them entirely. If you don't maintain a report of your work achievements, you might recall some by:

Looking at your closing appraisal.

Asking colleagues for feedback

Reviewing your work emails to locate examples from your clients or line supervisor.

You'll strengthen your answer by speaking out how your success benefited your employer.

For the first-class answers, use the STAR interview approach – situation, task, action, and result. How no longer to answer

Don't pick anything that isn't applicable to the function – or something that isn't a large achievement.

Do not be dishonest. Your claims will, in all likelihood, be fact-checked as part of the orientation procedure.

Don't be terrified to be gratified of something you've achieved. Self-assurance is conceivable except being cocky.

This query is also phrased as

What is your biggest achievement?

What is your greatest accomplishment?

Tell me about your biggest achievement.

What are you most proud of?

11. Why do we need to employ you?

What the employer needs to distinguish

The vital part of this question is 'you'. That's who the employer is concerned about.

What makes you qualified for the position? What are you influenced by?

See also: 4 What can you carry to the corporation?

Do you think you can offer us anything that other applicants can't?

How to answer

Replying a question like this capacity explaining your Unique Selling Prepositions (USPs) in particular.

Typical USPs include:

- You're skilled in the use of a specific tool, software or service.

- Your cutting-edge enterprise has put you on management training.

- You're licensed or possess a famed qualification.

- You're trained in fitness and safety or first aid.

Use questions like this to go past surely listing your abilities and definitely exhibit the lookup you've carried out on the enterprise and the functional requirements. Talk about how your unique skills can make a difference to the corporation and the challenges it faces.

This question gives you the opportunity to supply your elevator pitch. Have this snappy precis up your sleeve. Visualize, you are trapped in an elevator with the hiring supervisor – you be in a position to effortlessly pitch yourself with the key factors you'd wish to choose.

How not to reply

Whatever you do, don't say "I dont know."

Although you need to promote yourself, avoid answers that sound arrogant. Layout the statistics as an alternative than being big-headed about your experience and skills.

Avoid using clichés, also. Don't say you are zealous about the job. It's a very cliched time period that doesn't surely tell me anything. Try no longer to use generalist terms that ought to refer to whatever in life, not simply this role.

12. What can you offer that other applicants can't?

What the organization desires to know

Employers ask this query to:

Understand your character.

See if you're terrible about others.

See if you center of attention on yourself.

Find out whether or no longer you can cope under stress the question put you.

See also: 4 What can you deliver to the company? 6. What are your strengths? And 11 Why need to we appoint you?

How to answer

The enterprise is interviewing humans who they trust may want to do the job, so make positive you stand out. It could be you have an aggregate of skills or have performed a similar role.

Ask yourself: What do I have to give that others don't? Make a listing of your strengths and take a word of them into the interview with you.

These can be technical or behavioral skills. You may be any individual who excels at leading a team or has an effect and have an impact on at a govt level. Concentrate on these and go to the meeting outfitted with instances of how you have applied these and the quantifiable outcome. Where conceivable, provide numbers to delineate the results of your activities.

In case you're battling to think of a model, strive to suppose of time at a previous job, the place you exceeded your manager's expectations.

How not to answer

Don't make flimsy promises like "I've obtained hundreds of potentials" or "I'll provide this job 110%."

Provide tangible examples of your experiences or competencies. For example, don't say: "I went above and beyond what's it takes." Do say: "On task X, I went above and beyond what was required in Y and Z ways."'

Don't be poor about the organization you're interviewing for, such as pointing out loads of their flaws. Avoid being bad about your modern-day employer, too.

This question can be phrased as follow:

Why do you think you are the right candidate for for the job?

Why should we employ you?

13. What would you do within the first month of employment?

What the agency wants to know

The agency wishes to see if you have something that you'd like to acquire in the role.

They'll desire to establish whether or not you recognize what would be required of you, and how you'd make a contribution to the organization.

Employers additionally use this query to weed out candidates who aren't serious about getting the job.

See, additionally, 9. What would a first-rate performance look like in this role?

How to answer

The key is to show you understand the scope and nature of the company and to assure the employers that you're up for the challenge.

Prepare some goals, each with a timescale for execution. Make sure the goals and timelines are realistic yet realizable.

Goals should be personal, for your team, the commercial enterprise characteristic or for the business as a whole.

When you define your vision, demonstrate the experience and information you will deliver, however, also ensure that you are open-minded enough to research from, and react positively to the group that you are about to join. As experts, we frequently wish to make our mark as quickly as we can. However, it's essential to recognize the mounted working practice of your new crew adequate to learn the history and evolution first.

Don't claim you'll make an immediate impact. Savvy employers comprehend new hires can solely begin to have a significant effect in their second or 1/3 months in the role. The first month is frequently spent getting up to speed.

Make your reply unique to the job you've utilized for.

If you're making use of a challenge management role, your first most crucial intention would possibly be to entire your first venture inside the first three months.

For a workplace manager, your goal in the first week ought to be to learn the department's main systems and processes.

Maximize your lookup on the employer. For example, if they're about to carry a new product to market, relate your dreams to the launch.

The usage of a presentation is one of the exceptional approaches to speaking your deliberate impact. If you claim you have a presentation organized that you would like to take them through, it would honestly make you outstanding.

Those applying for senior and managerial roles must include their goals for the second year in the role. Such foresight signals your commitment and loyalty and underscores your strategic thinking.

How not to answer

Don't make up something on the spot. Get ready models ahead of time. Try not to make excessively driven cases, for example, 'I can turnaround this ineffectively performing office in about fourteen days.'

At long last, similarly, as with all inquiries, don't state "I don't have any acquaintance with." You won't land the position with that form of an answer, because it suggests to the organization that you don't care or that you're no longer capable.

This question is can also be put like this: What are you going to do in the first week of the job?

What would you do in the first yr in the job?

14. What form of surroundings do you like best?

What the company desires to know

The company wishes to know if you would in shape with its organizational lifestyle and working conditions. That includes:

Fitting in with the team.

Demographics and personalities of present employees.

Working hours.

Work ethic.

The administrative center (especially applicable for office jobs)

The agency isn't looking for a best in shape – just a true one. They're aware of imparting the job to anyone who wouldn't revel in working with them.

Equally, you shouldn't be given a job somewhere you know you won't be happy.

Do your lookup before the interview to get a proper grasp of the employer's lifestyle and environment. Don't vacillate to ask the company about it at some point in the interview: Candidates ought to continually understand it's a two-way conversation. It's vital to make sure the company's lifestyle matches them as lots as they fit the company. That will make for a profitable and happy candidate.

How to answer

Be candid about who you are and what you want. Candidates no longer take a function where they are aware that they will be unhappy, so it is not a terrible component, to be honest. If they are not happy to appoint you then they won't – and its capability you're now not an excellent fit.

It's very vital to do your research and to attempt and understand a bit greater about the culture of the company. It's one aspect to know about the information of the company; however, every other to comprehend what the tradition is like. Is it made up of very relaxed, younger, hippie, contemporary people? Is it a bit formal, a bit old fashioned? You' to try and make sure that in the same way they're attempting to provide you with a job, you're comfortable with the working environment.

When you research a prospective employer, be sure to consider what it's like to work there? Why do you prefer to work for us?). Understand the company's tradition by surfing the company's website, social media pages, and LinkedIn profiles of its present-day employees. It's also a good idea to search online for videos of the offices. If you know any present employees, see if you can speak to them. If you suppose you'd be a proper fit, spell out in your reply how your persona suits the company's core value.

How not to reply

You shouldn't lie to yourself or to the employer. If at interview, the company tells you about their work environment, and you recognize straight away that it wouldn't swimsuit you, say so. The interview would possibly very well cease there, so with courtesy, thank the interviewer for their time. They'll be grateful for your honesty.

It's a mistake to repeat the employer's internet site portrayal of their work atmosphere. Word-for-word recurrence will be noticeable to the interviewer, and they'll be left with the effect that you're no longer honest.

Don't center your attention on any negative thing about the employer's environment, for instance, the dated layout of the building or lack of interviewing rooms. In all likelihood, these are matters that frustrate your interviewers, and they don't want to hear about

it.

15. What's your dream job?

What the organization needs to distinguish

This is one of the difficult common interview questions to reply.

Not solely do you need to reply to the question that's explicitly asked; however, you've additionally obtained to answer any implied questions such as 'What's your profession path?'

Other indirect questions are:

What are your ambitions?

Do your ambitions align with the opportunities this company can offer?

Would you align with the company's core value?

How motivated are you for this job?

How pleased would you be in this job?

Employers like this question because it tests candidates by putting them under pressure. It often displays candidates who are not going to be loyal in the quick to medium term.

How to reply

Speak on:

The skills you acquire and how they meet the needs of the employer.

Those competencies you desire to develop and how this role will allow you to promote them are necessary. The beliefs and ideas that motivate you and how the enterprise is striving for them. Your areas of interest or passion and how this role will help you cope with them.

Your values and how nicely they align with those of the company.

One strategy is to talk about the magnitude of your dream job, as a substitute than a particular job title. "For example, maybe it's working with a progressive company or as part of a high-performing team. Think about what's vital to you and describe how your dream job aligns with this.

It's good enough to have hope and high aspirations at an early stage in your career, as long as you can show you're thinking about your career path. You may want to say: 'This job that I'm currently interviewing for is genuinely best in regards to giving me the abilities and skills required for the career route I'm on'.

In this case, talk about how the role you're applying for will enable you to develop in ways that'll assist your chosen career path.

It's essential to have some relevance for jobs in the enterprise that you're interviewing for. Whether it be in the science or finance field, it's important to link that dream job to the enterprise that you're applying for.

How not to reply

Avoid selecting a dream job that doesn't exist.

You ought to avoid straying too some distance from the function you're making use of for. Don't create an image so far removed from the job you're making use of for that it is unrealistic. List some key areas alternatively that your dream job would involve that marry up properly with the job you are making.

Don't point out something that should compromise your function if offered the job, such as working for a competitor, putting up your business, or touring the world.

Don't describe the job you're making use of for, because it'll sound like you lack drive.

CHAPTER EIGHT

Learn How to Interview your Prospective Employee

Many enterprise proprietors and hiring managers spend a lot of time interviewing, hiring and training new employees. It appears to be handy to select the proper man or woman for the job when candidates provide you with all the appropriate answers to your questions and score nicely on checks given in the process. Often times, though, as soon as they are employed, they show not to be the quality preference which ends up wasting a lot of your time and money. Effective questioning during the interview process will divulge the candidate's capacity to interact and talk in an unscripted way, therefore, revealing behaviors and data that will assist you in making higher hiring decisions.

Preparation before the interview; Always look at your resume before the interview and tailor it to the application and requirement of the company, if one is provided, to make sure the information is consistent. Resumes are simply a blueprint of experience; however, they can be used to decide a couple of necessary things before meeting the candidate. Determine if there is tenure in every position and steady work records with increasing responsibility. Usually, if their job titles exhibit less accountability as each position turns into an extra current, that is an indication that they are taking positions under their competencies for some reason, and that has to be addressed. Determine if the skills listed are both transferable to the function you are filling or precisely the experience wanted for the job.

Very often, employers only appear for capabilities concerning to their enterprise besides considering the possibilities of hiring any person with transferable capabilities that can bring a clear point of view to the position. Ensure that most of the resume is devoid of grammatical errors. If a resume is not proofread before it being sent out, most in all likelihood, the man or woman does not pay attention to elements, and that is a vital attribute with any new hire. If the resume has timelines that do not observe swimsuit or job descriptions and accomplishments that seem out of vicinity or unrealistic, then a set of questions about those problems must be noted and mentioned once the interview starts. Sometimes simply the clarification given by using the candidate is an eye-opener and sets the stage. Their motives for the inconsistencies will provide you with new records with insight to their professional and on occasion, personal background except immediately soliciting that information.

First impressions; It's continuously a desirable begin when an individual comes in searching professional and nicely groomed. A suit is expected to be worn if you are in a professional industry, unlike a blue-collar industry, where the gown code is extra casual. If they are poorly represented in their clothes so are you, then future customers and co-workers will have the same response that you have to their presence. A candidate that makes eye contact straight away and shakes your hand upon greeting you is a person that demonstrates confidence. When someone isn't in a position to present themselves with confidence, clients will now not have self-belief in them either. Being punctual is essential and ought to be noted. It shows that the candidate has responsible habits, which will subsequently relate to their future clients' first impressions as well. Professionalism, being punctual, exhibiting self-belief are all attributes employers look for in new hires, and they play an important function in the illustration of your company.

Gaining perception with high-quality questions; One of the largest errors employers can make when interviewing new candidates is to begin speaking about the function being provided too early in the process. Real questioning will allow the applicant to be published barring, giving them the ability to mold themselves to healthy the position. It's important to have interaction with the candidate with eye contact and allow them to have interaction with you within their relief degree first so that you can get more candid responses. Their body language, how they speak, and how they function themselves are all facts that offer you perception into how they deal with themselves. Explaining their past positions will exhibit you how they supply data as nicely as their presentation skills. Getting explanations of accomplishments at some point in their profession will make the difference between reciting their resume and getting examples of their results. Finding out how they get to the bottom of issues with clients and staff will exhibit you if they take the initiative in creating solutions and can turn a state of affairs around. These are the tell-tale questions that provide you with an insight into their problem-solving, client carrier or managerial style and communication skills.

Resumes can solely go such a way in giving you a clear picture of the candidate's capabilities. Getting them to disclose their actual selves is what you want when they are bodily in front of you. If they have had troubles with past supervisors and staff, it will come out in their responses and ought to be noted. Knowing their contemporary and previous compensation will inform you if they are earnings or commission pushed and what their comfort degree would be when touching on to your company's cutting-edge package. Growth is essential in business, and all of us can improve themselves in some area, so asking about that will disclose how they see themselves internally and will mirror in their actions, externally. I have gotten very straightforward solutions at instances to questions about their job preference over the current function being mentioned, which has guided my hiring decisions. It has kept me from placing the incorrect individual in a role that can doubtlessly waste treasured coaching time and money.

If they clearly don't have a passion for the position, they are making use of the opportunity to pursue something else however want a job right now, or are doing two things at once, you will find that outbarring at once asking about it. On the spot information, responses and reactions will show you the kind of worker you might have if you employed them. Standard HR questions like, "three adjectives that describe your personality" or "what are your strengths and weaknesses" and others that you had overcome. They take a look at the time so they are no longer going to supply you the exact photo of a person. They frequently come with rehearsed solutions given from textual content books, so having a more recent approach can furnish you with higher statistics to make the right hiring decisions. It is vital to continually document the responses given to your questions so you can assessment it in the future when finalizing, who is an excellent candidate for the position. Below is a guiding question that should be mixed with others that would help possibly current themselves as you go via the candidate's resume.

Explain your positions and experience on your resume within a 10 yr timeframe.

Give me examples of some of your biggest accomplishments all through your career?

What used to be your preferred position/ least favorite, and why?

Who was your fantastic supervisor, and why had been they the best?

Tell us a time when you dealt with an unhappy patron and how you resolved the issue?

The manager only: tell me about a time when you had a salesperson/employee that wasn't producing and what direction of action you took to flip around their productivity/work ethics?

The manager only: what is your management style, and how do you furnish coaching for your staff?

Manager only: how do you inspire your staff?

What have you completed in your previous positions to enhance your job know-how and or productivity?

What are your modern-day and previous compensation/quotas given and bonus opportunities achieved?

What do you think you can improve professionally?

Explain a time when you took the initiative to research something new in one of your positions?

What would be your dream job and career if you were in a position to pursue it, and why aren't you at this time?

Is there something you would like me to know about yourself that hasn't been mentioned thus far?

When would you be reachable to begin a new position?

Describing the position to be filled; This is a very important section of the process given that it will determine how the candidate views the role and your organization beyond the printed advertisement they responded to. The clarification has to be enticing, motivating and genuinely make the candidate excited about becoming a member of your team. Verbally explaining the business enterprise culture, work environment, pinnacle performers and boom possibilities available with enthusiasm need to be part of the dialogue over and beyond the job description. Company benefits are essential these days in attracting the proper candidates. You have to highlight the areas that are surprising when reviewing the health and the compensation sketch being presented for the position. Everyone wishes to work with any person that is advantageous and can encourage them, and this is your time to display these characteristics to them.

Qualifying their interest; So you are at the factor that you want to recognize how they see themselves in this position, what competencies they sense they have that is applicable to this position and what their level is in getting the role they are applying for. These questions will assist you in getting a higher understanding of if you have to pursue them or not if they stop up becoming your requirements. Often instances through asking these kinds of questions they will expose different records at this time that will help you in making the perfect decision. Seeing if they are enthusiastic about the function and if they can promote you on their talent set will allow you to decide if you prefer to take them into the subsequent step in the hiring process. If they do not display enthusiasm for the position and available job provides, then chances are they will act the same way in a day to day situation with customers and staff once they come aboard so, consider this.

Finalizing the interview; I continually like to hear the candidate ask, "What is the subsequent step"? Because they are attempting to close the interviewer and truly that is the kind of character a proprietor or hiring manager desires to convey aboard. Someone that takes the initiative is constantly a top thing whether or not they are in income or not. Explaining the hiring system of your organization will assist them in getting a higher understanding of the time body you have in filling the position. Asking candidates about what other positions they have applied for and if they are nevertheless pursuing any of them, will exhibit you what different possibilities are being to them. Knowing what other kinds of positions they are interviewing for will let you recognize if they are searching for remaining in their field, making a profession exchange or just attempting to get a job.

Still, you will attain a perception of their actual intentions for you to make higher hiring selections via positive questioning even when it relates to other companies. If there are different possibilities on the desk for them, you use this statistic wisely.

If you feel at the end of your time together that this may be the proper candidate for the position, then you can select to bodily walk them through the offices as they exit your company. Showing them around the office or just a place that they would possibly be working in and introducing them to some group of workers alongside the way will allow the candidate to visualize their region in your organization and can create a relief level inside that vision. Remember, it is still up to you to current your company, the function, and benefits in the most superb mild to seize the right candidate over your competition. Using this final step before they leave, if you are so inclined, can similarly add to their enthusiasm in trying the job and will impart a lasting impression. Nothing is guaranteed to be idiot-proof when interviewing and hiring employees, but being an effective interviewer is quintessential to your success charge and tenure of your staff. It will streamline the manner and help you recruit higher personnel with lasting results.

CHAPTER NINE

How to Manage Inappropriate or Interview Questions

As an applicant, you put a lot of energy into making your resume and cover letter and your networking your way to the ideal openings and managing your nerves on the day of the interview. You desire to make a correct influence with the aid of answering questions in a way that positions you like a sturdy applicant.

Now what do you do in the event the hiring supervisor poses inappropriate interview questions - or worse, illegal?

But unfortunately, there is no longer a hypothetical question. You may additionally be surprised to find out that in accordance with a survey conducted by Harris Poll, a surprising 20% of over 2,000 hiring and human aid managers that have been surveyed indicated they had asked a candidate illegal interview questions. When the same crew of hiring managers used to be with a list of illegal questions and they asked whether or not they had been legal, at least 33% said they weren't sure. Since you can't always remember the hiring managers to do the proper thing, getting to know this subject earlier than the big day can assist you in mapping out complicated boundaries.

Foremost, let's draw the mark on what unlawful interview questions are. In summary, race, gender, nationality, religion, navy status, marital status, and disability are all included categories. That ability employers cannot use them to discriminate in their hiring practices. That sounds reasonable, you would possibly say. In practical, what does that seem like? Below are a few examples of questions that are illegal all through the interview process. Some of them are so apparent you may cringe. Others are veiled and roundabout. You would possibly even spot one or two that you have been asked in an interview – I understand I did!

"Who will look after your kids during your working hours?"

A valid rule of thumb on any question that pointers at gender or household fame discrimination are to ask yourself, "Would the company be asking this if I had been the contrary sex? " The consequence in this question is that you may additionally not be capable of fulfilling the obligations of the job due to the fact you are a parent.

A legal way of asking this question would possibly seem like this: "Will you be handy to be available in the office from 8 to 6 in the course of the workweek?" As long as that is a legitimate job requirement, and the query is asked of each candidate, clarifying availability is a truthful game.

"Are you planning to have more children?"

Your family plans are legally off-limits in an interview, and this is an inappropriate interview question. While you may additionally be tempted to share being pregnant or little one stories with a hiring supervisor (especially if she comes throughout as friendly or has a photo of a younger child on her desk), the prudent factor to do is to refrain from doing so.

"How frequent are you absent for Army Reserve training?"

This is an instance of a discriminatory question primarily based on navy status. A criminal way of reframing this query is, "Are you available to tour two weeks out of the month to show off at conferences and visit clients?" If these are official job requirements.

"Have you ever been arrested?"

Asking about the arrest records of the candidate is an unlawful interview question. Notably, the hiring manager can ask whether or not you've ever been convicted of a crime or have used illegal capsules in the last three months, as neither crook conviction nor unlawful drug use is an endangered class.

"Are you on medication?"

This can be seen as an indirect method to get some information about your fitness history and feasible disability. A proper way to address the underlying issue is, "Are you healthy to function heavy machinery, as would be required with the aid of this job description?"

"Do you attend church every Sunday?"

This query tips at conceivable spiritual discrimination. A prison way to address a professional employment challenge is along the strains of, "Are you reachable for after-hours and weekend work obligation if needed?"

"What 12 months did you graduate from high school?"

This is simply any other way of asking how historical you are. Not OK.

Now that you understand what unlawful and inappropriate interview questions may seem like, what ought to your method be if one of these lands in your court? You have one of three choices.

Answer the question. Many candidates do this as a default, surely due to the fact they are afraid of coming throughout as non-collaborative or don't see whatever wrong with the question. My advice is to consider surely answering the query if you are at ease doing so. Short and candy solutions are best.

Refuse to reply to the question. With an inappropriate question, it is clearly inside your rights to now not answer it. You can point to the covered nature of the class as your motive for no longer responding. Most employers will come again off. Be prepared that this approach can create some awkwardness – not thru any fault of yours, but uncomfortable nonetheless.

Answer the intent of the question. This choice permits you to protect your rights and tactfully tackle the hiring manager's valid concern. You can offer a response that pursuits the heart of the question. In its place of answering, "Where were you born?" directly, you would possibly way "If you intended to ask whether I am legally allowed to work in the United States, the reply is yes." Alternatively, you ought to redirect with a clarifying question.

Your selections on an inappropriate interview query are surely the same as for an unlawful question. You can reply directly, use humor to redirect or ask the hiring manager to reveal how the query applies to the function you are applying for. If an illegal question makes you bitter on the position, reflect on consideration on it a blessing in hiding and fodder for a good story.

In closing, my high-quality advice, when dealing with unlawful and illegal interview questions, is to relax. In the course of the interview, as well as your professional life, you have manipulated over what takes place next. Don't let a prospective company bully you into disclosing something that you are now not blissful with.

Occasionally, hiring managers use unlawful questions as an intimidation tool. Most of the time, however, the interviewer might also now not recognize he is asking an illegal or an inappropriate question. This is especially real if an element of the interview is casual lunch with potential co-workers. Because of the comfy setting, it can be easy for them to slip into personal territory with you that would possibly be ordinary among them – however, it is not suitable with regards to the interview. Don't get cautious, ensure that you're in control and secure your non-open limits with elegance and certainty. Intend to diffuse the circumstance, and utilize this as a possibility to exhibit your interpersonal skills.

CHAPTER TEN

Types of Interview

Employers lead various types of job interviews, for example, case interview behavioral interviews, group interviews, online interview phone, and video interviews, second interviews, and even interviews held during a supper.

Those are significant job interviews to comprehend in case you're scanning for a job. However, there are different interviews you may understanding all through your vocation. These work-related interviews incorporate exit interviews, mock interviews, and informational interviews.

Behavioral Interviews

Interviewers utilize behavioral-based interviews to decide how you've taken care of different job circumstances before. The thought is that your past conduct predicts how you'll act in the new position. You won't get some simple "yes" or "no" questions and as a rule, you'll have to reply with an account about a past encounter.

Case Interviews

Interviews that incorporate the interviewer giving you a business situation and requesting that you deal with the circumstance are called case interviews. They're frequently utilized in the executive counseling and speculation banking interviews and expect you to flaunt your scientific capacity and critical thinking aptitudes.

Competency-Based Interviews

Interviews that expect you to give instances of explicit abilities are called competency-based interviews, or job explicit interviews. The interviewer will pose inquiries that will assist them in deciding whether you have the requirement and skills needed for a particular job.

Exit Interviews

An exit interview is a gathering between an employee who has surrendered or been fired and the organization's Human Resources office. Organizations lead these types of interviews, so they can become familiar with the workplace and land position criticism. You might be inquired as to why you found employment elsewhere, for what reason are you taking a new position, and what might you change about your job. These tips will assist you in dealing with an exit interview so you can proceed onward smoothly.

Final Interview

The final interview is the last advance in the interview procedure and the last interview you see if or not you'll find a new line of work offer. This kind of interview is usually directed by the CEO or different individuals from the upper administration. The way into a final interview is to pay attention to it as all the starter interviews — because you were approached in for a final interview doesn't mean you landed the position yet.

Group Interviews

Employers may hold group interviews since they're frequently more productive than face to face interviews. There are two major types of group interviews: one includes a candidate being interviewed by a group (or panel) of interviewers; the different includes one interviewer and a group of candidates.

Casual Interviews

Contracting supervisors may start the screening procedure with an informal, casual discussion rather than a proper interview. This is all the more an easygoing exchange than a run of the mill job interview. On a comparable note, a visit over some espresso is another less popular sort of job interview.

Informational Interview

An informational interview is utilized to gather data about a job, vocation field, industry or organization. In a situation like this, you're the interviewer and you discover individuals to talk with so you can become familiar with a particular field.

Lunch and Dinner Interviews

One reason employers accept position up-and-comers out on a brief siesta or supper is to go through their social abilities and to check whether they can deal with themselves nimbly under strain. Recall that despite everything you're being watched so utilize your best social graces, pick nourishments that aren't excessively untidy.

Mock Interviews

A mock interview furnishes you with a chance to rehearse for an interview and get input. Even though you can do a casual mock interview with a family member, a mock interview with a lifelong mentor, guide or college vocation office will give the best criticism.

Off-Site Interviews

Employers once in a while plan job interviews in an open spot, similar to a café or eatery. Maybe there is no neighborhood office or perhaps they don't need current employees to think about the probability of another contract. Regardless, it's great to be prepared for off-site interviews.

On the Spot Interview

Now and then you'll be relied upon to do an on the spot interview. For instance, you may turn in your application and be approached to do an interview immediately. Or on the other hand when an association (ordinarily retail or cordiality) reports they will hold open interviews on a particular date. In circumstances like these, enlisting staff use on-the-spot interviews to screen candidates and promptly choose who ought to and ought not to be remembered for the following stage of the enrolling procedure.

Panel Job Interview

A panel job interview happens when you're interviewed by a panel of interviewers. You may meet with each panel part independently or all together. What's more, now and again, there will be a panel of interviewers and a group of up-and-comers across the board room.

Phone Interviews

While you're job looking, you should be prepared for a phone interview on a minute's notice. Organizations frequently start with an unscheduled phone call, or perhaps you'll get the opportunity to plan your call. In either case, it's great to be prepared and prepared to ask phone interview inquiries to ask the interviewer too.

Second interview

You passed your first interview and you got a call or email to plan a second interview. This interview will increase point by point and might last for few hours.

Organized Interview

An organized interview is regularly utilized when an employer needs to survey and contrast you and competitors in a fair-minded way. The interviewer asks every one of the up-and-comers similar inquiries. If the position requires explicit aptitudes and experience, the employer will draft interview addresses concentrating precisely on the capacities the organization is looking for.

Unstructured Interviews

An unstructured interview is a job interview in which questions might be changed based on the interviewee's reactions. While the interviewer may have a couple of set inquiries prepared ahead of time, the heading of the interview is somewhat easygoing, and questions stream is based on the bearing of the discussion. Unstructured interviews are frequently observed as less scary than formal interviews.

Video Interviews

Maybe you've gone after a virtual position or you're interviewing for a situation in another state (or nation). Programming projects, for example,

Skype, Zoom, and FaceTime making video calling simple and video interviews are getting popular.

CHAPTER ELEVEN

Importance of Job Interview

Job interview is one of the important occasions in one's life. On the off chance that it is your first, the importance increments. How can one force it off without anxiety or dread? One of the key things individuals overlook when they go into an interview is that staying cool is the best alternative. Be loose and prepared, the best answers will come alone. What is the fear all about when all the information you ever need has now been given to you?

Regularly, individuals lose in the interview since they are terrified at last. For what reason does this occur? All things must be considered when you are pondering on what's to come. The preeminent idea going through our brains before the interview is that on the occasion that we don't succeed, at that point what will occur? Where will I land the following position? These negative considerations make us apprehensive and empower to address the least complex of inquiries. So being certain is a significant point before setting off to a job interview

Before the interview, might be a day earlier, make sure to rationally practice the interview from your very own point of view: When you are satisfied with the envisioned exhibition you are delivering, step inside the picture of yourself and go through the situations again as though you are presently doing it. It couldn't be any more obvious, feel and hear it as though it is indeed occurring. This time, you are watching out into the world from your own eyes, so your arms are straightforwardly before you with individuals confronting you, as you feel your garments on your body. Enable everything to unfurl in incredible detail - make it as genuine as conceivable by giving your creative mind a chance to allowed to have a vibrant and brilliant perspective on a fruitful day. Finally, give extraordinary consideration again to sentiments, truly invest energy envisioning yourself feeling precisely how you need to feel, and afterward go land the position! Visualizing your prosperity can get you precisely that. On the off chance that you consider negative things, at that point, you will undoubtedly get that.

Like anything in life it requires some investment to get great at mental practice. Utilizing this representation strategy for twenty minutes daily will prepare your cerebrum to perform new practices. The outcomes will surprise you. Judgemental practice by giving it a shot in life. Decide by yourself how feasible it is. Use it to prepare for those significant job interviews and appreciate the fulfillment that originates from realizing that you are performing at your absolute best.

In the long run, you will have the option to utilize this methodology in everyday circumstances spontaneously by concentrating on utilizing the intensity of your creative mind. A creative mind is the blessing an individual has. Use it today for your prosperity and the venturing stone to another future with more brilliant possibilities!

Essentially, one can't take somebody he/she just met into his residence legitimate examination or truth-finding to think twice about it in the future. Same additionally applies for companies, enlistment offices and employers as they might want to examine and research any individual who is intrigued and qualified in going along with them, the imminent candidates vocation aspirations, ways of thinking and objectives must coordinate with the organization's key objectives and targets with the goal for work to happen after the interview process.

Companies and enrollment offices place extraordinary importance on interviews, as they are genuinely keen on getting precise and basic data about the applicants and settled a decent affinity with the imminent employees. Most employers settle different terms of work with their prospective employees during the interview procedure. Most companies, considerably in the wake of leading arrangement of composed assessments and fitness test for their candidates still apply oral interview at the last phase of the enrollment procedure before business is offered to the competitor. I once went for an interview, and one of the inquiries the interviewer posed to me was on the off chance that I knew why I have required the interview. The Interviewer might likewise want to sell the organization and her picture, including some hidden costs to the candidate with the goal for them to know why it is fundamental for them to know why they need to get utilized by the organization.

Companies and employers are having more than the necessary number of qualified candidates for a specific job resort to job interview with the end goal for them to deal with those up-and-comers best qualified and appropriate for the job and spot them into different divisions and areas inside the association. Another basic motivation behind why companies direct interviews for imminent employees is to pass judgment and assess the appropriateness of the contender for the job, putting together this for the job and related job requirement labor prerequisites.

Candidates and job searchers need to, as a matter of high importance, place significant accentuation on job interviews as it is the fundamental factor that decides their business appropriateness by the organization or association they are applying to.

CHAPTER TWELVE

What to Wear to a Job Interview

For a long time, the standard counsel I give to job-seekers about what to wear for a job interview is"Dress just like you already have the job." There are organizations where everyone wears shorts and flip-flops to work. There are many others where ladies still need to wear skirts - and I'm discussing employers in the U.S.

There are companies where people must wear suits to work every day. A coat, tie and pants are not proper in those places. It must be a suit. You probably won't think about a company dress code. I believe you have attended many interviews in a blazer and did not eventually land the position - and never know why.

On the other hand, you probably won't need the job, on the off chance that you think the dress code is excessively formal.

There are organizations where individuals can wear slacks or skirts with or without blazers. However, ladies must wear hose on their legs.

Exposed legs are not permitted, in any event, for long skirts that touch the floor.

Each company is unique. How might you realize what to wear to a job interview before you arrive and perceive how individuals are dressed?

Today In: Leadership

You need to inquire!

You will get an email message or a phone call from a selection representative or an organization HR individual, or maybe from one of its chiefs, welcoming you to a job interview. Here are the means by which that correspondence will look:

Dear James,

A debt of gratitude is in order for the visit you took to my office a few evenings ago to inquire about our Financial Analyst position. Our Controller, Harry Jones, might want to meet with you to speak further about the position. Would you be able to be with us here at our office on Thursday, November seventh at 4:00 p.m.? You'll be here for around two hours. Let me know whether that date works for you and have an amazing day.

Yours,

Annette Barnes

Zenith Explosives Recruiter

Here's your answer:

Dear Annette,

Much obliged, especially for your message, I'd be glad to meet Harry Jones on Thursday, November seventh at 4:00 p.m. at your office. Would you be able to please prompt me on the suitable dress for an interview with your firm? Much obliged especially ahead of time,

Yours,

James Brown

Annette will do as well as can be expected. However, it's difficult to expressly state dress codes. That is one explanation I prompt HR individuals never to attempt! Dress codes are social. They move after some time and with the seasons. Regardless of what Annette exhorts you, do your own examination also.

Take a look at the same number of LinkedIn profiles for Acme Explosives colleagues as you can. Look at their administrators, accurately, and scan the Acme site for photographs of the top individuals there just as different photographs of the employees at work.

On the off chance that the Acme dress code is generally good, take it up an indent for your job interview.

The typical office clothing is khakis and polo shirts, wear a conservative shirt and a fine coat for your interview, with a tie. On the off chance that you appear and feel you're overdressed, you can generally remove the tie in the men's room and put it in your pocket.

If the typical office clothing is a creator suit with a handkerchief, at that point, wear that to your job interview.

If the typical official wear is pants and awesome teeshirts, wear a traditional shirt and khakis with no tie.

The accept it-up-a-score counsel is the equivalent for ladies. If the ladies at your future employer wear sundresses with spaghetti ties and jam shoes to work, go to the interview wearing a casual dress or slacks with some sort of topper, similar to a little sweater or a casual coat.

If the employees wear naval force slacks and silk shirts with pearls to work, dress a similar route for your job interview.

I got notification from an advertisement office VP one time that he needed to employ a sharp youthful planner for his firm. However, the architect went to the job interview in dress pants and a white shirt with a tweed coat. The advertisement office VP said he couldn't procure somebody who dressed that way, regardless of how gifted he may be.

I told the VP I imagined that was the most idiotic thing I had ever heard. How was the planner expected to think about your arbitrary fashion inclinations? I asked him. I'll wager that the creator has his very own firm now and is doing splendidly.

Now and again, individuals come to job interviews feeling somewhat overdressed and afterward, from that point forward, they come to consequent interviews and gatherings with the employer dressed calmly. That is alright, yet I don't prescribe that you take it excessively far.

Our companion Philip had a third interview with an authority group. They were meeting for supper at a steakhouse in New York. You can wear pants and a tee-shirt to a steakhouse, yet for what reason would you? It was as yet a job interview. Philip wasn't thinking.

He went to the steakhouse in pants and a teeshirt with a cowhide coat. The officials were there in business clothing.

"Our misstep," they said. "We thought this was a business arrangement."

Philip realized he had blown it. His brain hustled. He said, "I'm sorry to wear the wrong cloth for this interview. That was an awful pass on my part. If you feel that it's simply not a fit, I'm glad to allow you to continue ahead with your nighttimes. I would prefer not to go through your time." The officials regarded that. They enlightened him not to stress concerning it.

"We're going to contact you," they said. "Try to dress suitably for business capacities." Then everybody left. Philip had an extraordinary supper and found an incredible new line of work.

In any occasion that you sense the nearness of an obvious issue at hand, it's in every case preferred to refer to it over to keep quiet!

Consider your interview clothing before the enormous day or the prior night. Prepare everything including your shoes, socks, and underwear, and check your clothes for spots, string pulls, or indications of wear. You need to feel incredible on your interview, and looking extraordinary is a major piece of that!

Wear hues that look incredible on you. Ensure you can take them! In case you're wearing a skirt, work on plunking down in it to ensure that when you're situated, you're not blazing a lot of flanks and diverting the interviewer from the discussion. Ensure your underwear ties don't appear.

I favor shut toed siphons or pads to open-toed shoes for ladies. However the world is changing and on the off chance that you believe I'm excessively stodgy, at that point, pursue your dream. On the off chance that you wear open-toed shoes, get a pedicure before the interview!

If you like to wear cosmetics and gems, put it all on the line. It's you going on the interview, and you in person is a major piece of your image. I don't need you to change who you are for the job interview. In such a case that you do that then the company is going to have a wrong opinion of you.

It's up to you. A few associations will adore you and some will despise you regardless of what your identity is or how you dress, so there's no utilization attempting to crush yourself into a crate for another person's accommodation or solace.

That being stated, the more 'unprofessional' your look, the less the companies that are probably going to get you. That may approve of you! If they don't get you, they don't merit you, regardless of whether you are a buttoned-down corporate person as far as possible or Creative Colorful Person.

We offer ideal guidance in our training, yet I have just at any point offered spontaneous closet guidance once. I was addressing a crowd of people of job-searchers and a man of his word moved toward me after my discussion. He was an exceptionally decent fifty-something individual with grinning blue eyes and his unique pilot conceals from the seventies.

The pilot glasses had a messed up outline that was taped closed on the extension of the refined man's nose. "I heard that pilot glasses are back in style," he said to me regarding nothing. I figured he needed my supposition. "Almost certainly they are," I stated, "yet not excessively combine - you need to get new glasses."

"That is actually what my significant other says!" said the respectable man. "Savvy lady," I said.

Regardless of whether you're a man or a lady, ensure your shoes are spotless and sparkled and give strolling a shot a hard floor in them, to ensure they don't squeak or make a boisterous commotion. That would be awkward for you, and you needn't bother with any more worry than the commonplace job interview gives without anyone else.

Choose what you're wearing to the job interview and take care of your interview outfit in a sheltered spot in your storeroom where your children can't spill anything on it. Rise right off the bat interview day and wash up. You will be splendid, and they're going to adore you. We should trust the individuals you meet are deserving of your abilities!

Things that are not good to wear to a job interview

A major some portion of finding a new line of work is establishing a decent first connection, and a major some portion of establishing a decent first connection is the way you dress for the interview. While you don't need to spend a great deal of cash on your closet, placing in some additional exertion will satisfy over the long haul. Before your next interview, ensure you aren't committing any interview clothing errors.

01

Keep Bright, Flashy Colors to a Minimum

While everybody realizes that short hemlines and diving neck areas aren't satisfactory for a job interview, wearing an improper dress that is likewise a splendid, conspicuous shading, similar to red, basically exacerbates things.

Along these lines, be careful when picking your clothes. In case you're going to wear a tight-fitting, cloth or pronounced color do it thoughtfully, ensuring the general plan of your outfit is particularly traditionalist. Different colors are less emotional that function admirably for business interviews. What's more, it's a smart thought to evade short hemlines and skin-tight fits, see-through and uncomfortable cloth.

2.

Blazer Doesn't Complement All Outfit

While a blazer is a decent go-to decision for practically any interview, be aware of what you wear underneath. The profound v shape formed by the blazer's lapel makes a diving neck area. In case you're going to wear a nightgown or a shell underneath, ensure it covers you suitably. Layering with a conservative is a no-bomb choice, as well.

This tip applies to men, as well. Except if you're interviewing in a simple sector or business, as at a new business, wearing a blazer on top doesn't give you the reason to wear a shirt underneath. Put more effort and where a conventional yet professional dress to your interview.

CHAPTER THIRTEEN

How to manage Anxiety Interview

There are three basic times in the job interview process when we can be really worried: before the interview, during the interview, and after the interview are the periods we get worried. As I have broad understanding of this procedure from the two sides of the work area and from talking about this circumstance with customers throughout the years; I will presently proceed to examine valuable systems that can help get over worry in these circumstances.

BEFORE THE JOB INTERVIEW

There are numerous worries than can emerge here from delayed stress making us become tired and experience the ill effects of poor focus to a minute ago hurrying - something that can prompt a lot of pressure.

• PLAN WELL AHEAD: As it is a smart thought to do some foundation investigation into the job, the organization and more extensive industry; leaving a lot of time to do this is a smart thought. Hurrying and packing data in the previous night prompts worry as well as just adds to our present moment, instead of long haul, memory - leaving us increasingly inclined to overlook these important details when required.

• MAKE SURE TO GET PLENTY OF REST: This is mostly as a decent night rest. While this contrasts for all of us, the suggested measure of rest every night for the average individual is around 8 hours. Not exclusively is getting this lay significant on the night before the interview yet additionally during the time from when we realize we have the interview. Lying in bed around evening time and pondering the interview - or some other stresses so far as that is concerned - will discourage us from getting the necessary rest. Undoubtedly, if this happens after quite a while after night, our wellbeing will likewise endure, close by our degrees of indispensable fixation required for the interview.

• LEAVE PLENTY OF TIME BEFORE THE INTERVIEW TO GET READY AND ARRIVE AT THE INTERVIEW VENUE: Rushing before an interview is one of the most unpleasant things that we can do. As being late for an interview is likely one of the most serious interview messes up we can make; surging will cause incredible uneasiness. My best appeal here is to rise from the get-go the morning of the interview. Eat a substantial and healthy breakfast (and lunch if the interview is in the late evening), however not over the top measures of nourishment as this can prompt inconvenience and tiredness, and enable a lot of time to prepare. It is also a smart thought to go out earlier than we would somehow or another for a similar trip to permit this additional time - and to land at the interview setting early. At the point when I state early, I intend to state around 10 minutes before the interview time. Too soon can be as off-putting as past the point of no return and sitting hanging tight for the interview can make us become pushed. If we do show up before the expected time, it is ideal to go for a short walk around the neighborhood, in the shops or have a calm plunk down. Whatever occurs, make an effort not to get worked up. Perusing some organization limited time material while holding back to be welcomed for the interview can enable us to unwind - and shows that we are keen on the organization/association.

DURING THE INTERVIEW

Similarly as with any job interview each second tallies here, with stress being the feeling that is unhelpful in this circumstance.

• MEET THE INTERVIEWER AND WALK SLOWLY AND CALMLY INTO THE ROOM: This is one of those occasions where stress can emerge in a flash absent much by way of caution. We may grope genuinely quiet until this point yet when we stroll through the entryway and see the interviewer(s) before us, the pressure can hit us like a block divider. This likewise will, in general, be when individuals surge - hurrying through the entryway and plunking down straight away without a presentation - especially etiquette for an interview! Strolling gradually and smoothly into the room, taking genuinely full breaths (in through the mouth and out by means of the nose) can be a decent method for not 'reaching this stopping point of pressure.' This will likewise cause us to appear to be increasingly proficient and certain.

• LISTEN CAREFULLY AND THINK BEFORE ANSWERING ANY QUESTIONS: This may sound clearly self-evident, yet when seemingly out of the blue this exhortation can at times be overlooked.

Particularly in these types of circumstances, we regularly hear what we need to hear and not what has really been inquired. Addressing an inappropriate inquiry can complete two things: (an) it can cause us to appear to be indiscreet - not great during a job interview, and (b) it can detrimentally affect the entire interview. For example, we may understand halfway that we are addressing an inappropriate inquiry or not noting appropriately. This would then be able to make us stop, lose our focus and lead to lost certainty - which is hard to get in a short space of time. As the customary saying goes 'a line in time spares nine', implying that it is smarter to require some investment and afterward (getting things right) as opposed to surging and committing errors (making more work and worry for ourselves). I have consistently been intrigued by individuals in interviews who have really had the mental fortitude to state they didn't hear the inquiry appropriately and pose on the off chance that I could rehash it.

• PLACE SOMETHING ON THE DESK TO HOLD OR REFER TO: It abandons saying here this ought to be something profoundly significant to the job interview. It can frequently be an excellent thought to put a journal, special material (shows inquire about aptitudes) or scratchpad on the work area before us. The brilliant principle here is to consistently ask the interviewer(s) consent before doing this - albeit most occasions, they will be glad to oblige and may really be intrigued as this additionally shows duty and association. Likewise, request to take notes. Again this shows intrigue, certainty and from a pressure viewpoint can take our brain of the worry by glancing down at the paper and accomplishing something physical, for example, composing. Putting these things around us - obviously enables us to feel somewhat responsible for our condition and this thus can help diminish pressure.

AFTER THE INTERVIEW

This is a period that is frequently not talked about however like the interview itself can be unpleasant. The primary pressure made here is brought about by leaving the interview room and building and afterward the hanging tight for the news affirming or dismissing us for the job. While there is little we can do at this phase to change the result of the interview or the operations of HR divisions; this pressure can detrimentally affect us and our future interviews - mainly if a past dismissal from our interview seriously constrains our certainty.

• ON LEAVING THE INTERVIEW ROOM, LEAVE SLOWLY AND CALMLY: I can't disclose to you the occasions I have interviewed individuals where the interview has gone genuinely well yet they have been in a focused on alarm toward the conclusion to leave the room. This surge frequently brings about a poor withdrawing impact for the interviewer yet, in addition, can prompt mishaps. Often, the last impression an individual makes in an interview can be as significant as the first and a poor last impression may offset the first. I once interviewed an individual who was in such a hurry to leave the interview room, that they thumped some tea everywhere throughout the work area, including my notes. I have additionally known about a woman in such a hurry to leave, that she left the room by means of an inappropriate entryway - strolling into a capacity cabinet. To stay away from this, toward the finish of the interview, after the entirety of the inquiries, etc, attempt to trade minor merriments, gradually gather the entirety of your assets and warmly greet everybody in the room. In all likelihood in an interview, we will be appeared out of the space to the primary passageway of the structure. Here, simply be regular and make minor casual discussion - show that you are human and have a character. While the interviewers might be in a race to see the following interviewee, be genuinely fast, don't defer them and yet don't surge and certainly not freeze. Loosen up when outside the structure and out of scope of the interviewers.

• TRY NOT TO ANALYZE THE INTERVIEW ONCE IT IS OVER: At this phase, there is presently nothing that should be possible to change information exchanged in the interview, so regardless of how hard it is, there is little point breaking down it - despite the fact that this is enticing. Irrespective of how well or how gravely we feel the interview went, we will consistently discover flaws on the off chance that we start examining it. This can likewise prompt further unhelpful pressure. On the off chance that we are educated that we have not been acknowledged for the job, it is significant not to lose certainty. This can prompt further pressure and can thus negatively affect our business possibilities for what's to come.

These are only a few methods that have I have recommended to customers throughout the years - because of past encounters. While there are some more, these ought to go far to decrease worry in job interviews. As I have appeared in the article, it isn't only the job interview itself that can be unpleasant yet additionally the arrangement and time following the interview - sitting tight for the outcomes. I trust these strategies will help in future interviews and wish everybody going after another position the absolute best of karma and achievement later on.

Getting an interview is an energizing and significant advance in getting employed. The interview will be centered around a discussion planned for finding progressively about your character, aptitudes and capabilities. Imparting great during your interview is a basic piece of the procedure and will enable you to get the best enlisted.

CHAPTER FOURTEEN

How to face an Interview

It is crucial to be proficient and sure. They watch ranges of abilities, yet besides, they check non-verbal communication.

Try not to look stressed in the interview, be cool to face the interview. Everyone needs to do is go with the correct frame of mind and be fruitful.

Try not to make any imperfections out of strain. Indeed, even the interviewers check the job-seekers' clothing.

So one should spruce up well in an interview. Here are tips on how to face the interview.

How to tackle an interview for new job-seekers (fresher):

Interviews are precarious with regards to an individual who is a genuine fresher in the field and there might be a likelihood that a fresher can wind up look unusual or apprehensive during their interview and to defeat that circumstance a fresher needs to keep these things in his/her brain.

   1. Arrangement:

2. One ought to get prepared a long time before the interview, check every one of the endorsements and archives required for interview.

Prepare a resume with data simply required, don't destroy with all subtleties. Practice your presentation and right yourself if there are botches.

Take barely any subjects and prepare yourself for group talk round, this will truly assist you with performing in an interview well. There are a couple of generally asked questions in the interview, which a fresher needs to prepare to answer them.

2. Clothing:

Clothing assumes a crucial job when going to interviews. It makes a decent impression at his/her first look in an interview.

Employers do watch their appearance and they will know how proficient an up-and-comer in the workplace would be.

Even when you performed well in an interview, a bad dressing may make you lose a chance. So get prepared with formal dress before the interview.

Manage to show the best of yourself, which is in line with, and suitable for the interview.

3. The resume ought to be exact:

The first thing a selection representative watches is a competitor resume. This should cover all the significant ranges of abilities and encounters.

It must not be excessively long, sufficiently right. On the off chance that there are abilities that are useful and applicable to the association, this may be helpful to snatch openings in the company.

Make sure everything is referenced in the resume so that you won't be questioned further and inconvenience yourself.

4. Be reliable:

Try not to be late for an interview. Prepare a day prior with all the important courses of action to visit so you do no get late to the interview think about the drive time to arrive at the venue. You must have it in mind to arrive at the right time.

Late appearance demonstrates that you are unprofessional, carefree and reckless.

Arrive at the scene early with the goal that you will have the opportunity to comfort yourself in that spot. This decreases the strain and makes you feel ease.

5. Learn about the company before going to the interview:

It is important to think about the company information and what job you are going to play, how it precisely identifies with your capabilities.

Try to learn it from a friend if they are now an employee of that company. Employers may ask questions for what reason do they picked this field, how pertinent the job position to them, so it's important to be prepared for every answer.

Comprehend the work culture and attempt to dazzle the interviewers.

6. Conquer dread:

For fresher this may be the first interview, and perhaps this is great chance to substantiate yourself. So don't get tense and overpowered.

Be calm and patient, don't do anything to straighten something up. Your face must be covered with a smile at all times. You may answer questions wrongly when pressured still don't lose your temper.Sit firm and be mindful of your environment.

7. Fearlessness:

Answer everything with certainty. Go with an uplifting frame of mind and answer everything with confidence.

Your clothing, abilities, capabilities and arrangement are immaculate one can without much of a stretch face the interview.

Keep in touch with the interviewer don't occupy, don't shake legs or chomp nails simply be firm and expert. Break down the question appropriately and answer them with certainty.

8. Be straightforward:

Try not to give bogus data with respect to your aptitudes or experience. This may prompt lose a chance.

Be straightforward with your assessments and adaptable to the work environment condition. Ask questions on the off chance that you have any questions since they are the best individual to answer every one of the inquiries so you can be OK with the following hiring process.

This likewise shows your soundness to work in that association.

9. Demonstrate how better you are, than others:

Numerous candidates will go to the interview. So one ought to demonstrate that you are more remarkable than others.

Tell them how great you can fit into the company and how would you be able to help the development of the company and furthermore singular development.

Additionally, let them realize how energized you are functioning with that association.

How is the firm performing and about the firm work culture, and so on, this will tell you the selection representative that he/she is particularly intrigued to work with the association.

10. Know your qualities and shortcoming:

Employers may ask about competitor qualities and shortcomings. So prepare yourself and think about your capacities and potential.

Show every one of your qualities as they are ideal to get selected in the interview. Try not to say about your shortcomings which will prompt lose your chance.

11. Give a perfect pitch:

They do check relational abilities, which are important in a working environment. So prepare well with your presentation.

Try not to delay in center of your discourse. Continue chatting with a rich voice so every one of the people in the lobby can unmistakably comprehend your voice. Make it exact without avoiding important focuses.

Enable the interview to question, make him complete the sentence at that point answer it. Try not to talk about the components referenced in the resume, talk about things that must be raised to put in the interview.

12. Leave a card to say thanks while leaving:

Be gracious with the enrollment specialists, before leaving, say, "Thank you for giving this chance" or " decent chatting with you".

Regardless of whether it is fruitful or not, accept this open door as trying and face it. You may succeed or not, I am sure you will gain some new useful knowledge from this chance. That may help you in your next interview.

Dissect the slip-ups in the interview, and attempt to redress them and present yourself to face the following test.

13. Be certain with the criticism:

Once in a while, it happens that in the wake of going to an interview an applicant who can be considered as a fresher with regards to going to an interview may wind up encountering some awful stuff that might be a lower level of certainty and some terrible encounters.

For instance, when a fresher goes to an interview for a situation for which he/she has prepared certainly yet, in the long run, the interview turned out poorly as he/she expected and around then that up-and-comer may feel low about their first involvement with that company or association.

How to Face an Interview for Experienced Applicant:

Furthermore, when it comes to an accomplished competitor they should be sure about themselves and pursue beneath referenced things before going for any interviews.

1. Give a brief about Previous experience:

While you were asked to tell about yourself, quickly clarify about your past job and field in which you worked.

Tell them your track records in that company and how you adjusted work life. Additionally, the most significant accomplishment while working in a group.

Likewise, attempt to connect that involvement in this association in which you needed to get put. With the goal that interviewer may note it and you may score great to pass the interview.

2. Try not to condemn past employers:

Never talk seriously about the companies where you worked. Try not to reprimand them. Indeed, even you have an awful involvement with past company don't open up with the enrollment specialist.

This shows an individual's inspirational mentality towards the company, so never talk negative. This may likewise demonstrate that you will surrender things effectively.

Relax and consider prevailing in this interview, rather than losing the opportunity by speaking seriously about past association

3. Clarify your most grounded motivation behind why would you like to change into the new company:

Maybe you are working as of now for a company and you may go to an interview to work in the new company.

In that case, let the employers think about your points and objectives. How you needed to go through past achievement and knowledge and take a risk in the new company and develop in your vocation, likewise reveal to them how important this open door for you.

Don't raise your self-awareness; likewise, reveal to them how you are going to serve the company and satisfy your obligations.

4. Show of aptitudes and capacities:

An accomplished individual who has shown up in the majority of the interviews keeps up a level of correspondence where he/she can discuss better with the interviewer.

Most basic correspondence sources would be imparted through aptitudes and capacities. It is one of the important sources of correspondence where an applicant gets a chance to show their aptitudes and capabilities to the company or the recruiting agency.

5. Introduction of most extreme information:

An individual who is well versed and highly experienced in a field shows their best in that specific field when contrasted with others.

Battling for jobs and getting employed for a position are two unique things, these things appear to make a circumstance where a competitor attempts to clarify the interviewing panel about the valuable information about the field though nobody else can have that information.

6. Correspondence:

It is a ridiculous thing to clarify that an individual who has such degree of involvement with job interviews and such experience might want a career.changeAlso, in both circumstance, an individual who is involved an interview may have the option to deal with the interviewers by his/her correspondence level.

Conclusion

If you are searching for job interview success tips, you will achieve a lot from the information in this guide. Recall, a job interview is an assembly between a possible worker and a particular company that approves the guys and women worried to observe data on one another. Your cause as a viable worker is to show the strengths that you have that will make contributions to the business enterprise that you are in search of employment from in a great manner. You will represent the written archives that you have positioned on your resume. You will give your resume a good persona and character that are worthy. By using this manual you can be sure that you are going to ace the next job interview and secure the job that you have been invited to be interviewed for.

You, in all likelihood, already understand that an interview isn't just a hazard for the hiring supervisor to grill you with interview questions— it's your responsibility to find out whether or not a job is perfect for you. That means: It's vital to go to an interview with some questions to ask the interviewers. Doing that will enable you to make the final decision about the company and the position you are being offered. What do you prefer to know about the company? The company? The department? The team? To get you thinking, I have put a list of key questions collectively to ask in an interview the usage of the encouraging points of this eBook. We surely don't suggest asking all of them rapid-fire—some of this stuff will indeed be covered at some point in your discussion, and you can weave in different questions as you go. But when the unavoidable, "So, do you have a question for us?" section of the interview comes, use the ideas and likely questions discussed in this book and ensure you cover all bases. You should think critically about how you can differentiate yourself from others at every step of the way during the interview.

GOOD LUCK!